P9-ARU-531

34.50

75U

NEBUCHADREZZAR
AND BABYLON

Reconstruction of the ziggurat

NEBUCHADREZZAR
AND BABYLON

D.J. WISEMAN, F.B.A.

EMERITUS PROFESSOR OF ASSYRIOLOGY IN THE
UNIVERSITY OF LONDON

THE SCHWEICH LECTURES
OF THE BRITISH ACADEMY
1983

PUBLISHED FOR THE BRITISH ACADEMY
BY THE OXFORD UNIVERSITY PRESS
1985

DS
73.92
·W57
1985

Oxford University Press, Walton Street, Oxford OX2 6DP
London New York Toronto
Delhi Bombay Calcutta Madras Karachi
Kuala Lumpur Singapore Hong Kong Tokyo
Nairobi Dar es Salaam Cape Town
Melbourne Auckland
and associate companies in
Beirut Berlin Ibadan Mexico City Nicosia

Oxford is a trade mark of Oxford University Press

Published in the United States by Oxford University Press, New York
ISBN 0 19 726040 3
© *The British Academy, 1985*

All rights reserved. No part of this publication may be reproduced,
stored in a retrieval system, or transmitted, in any form or by any means,
electronic, mechanical, photocopying, recording, or otherwise, without
the prior permission of Oxford University Press

British Library Cataloguing in Publication Data

Wiseman, D.J.
Nebuchadrezzar and Babylon. — (Schweich Lectures
in Biblical Archaeology)
I Title   II British Academy   III Series
935′.04   DS 71
ISBN 0 19 726040 3

Produced by Alan Sutton Publishing, Gloucester
Printed in Great Britain

PREFACE

I wish to thank the President, Council and Schweich Committee of the British Academy for the honour shown me by the invitation to deliver this twenty-first series of Schweich lectures on Biblical Archaeology in 1983. It had been my original hope that these could provide a complete reevaluation of all the evidence for the reign of Nebuchadnezzar II of Babylon, (605–562 B.C.) from the inscriptions and archaeology as well as a study of the prosopography and economy of the period. The brief time available for preparing these lectures and other commitments, however, precluded this latter research which is essential for a more adequate picture to be presented.

The subject was chosen since the last days of Judah and the early period of the Jewish exile in Babylonia are crucial in ancient Near Eastern and Biblical studies. There is today renewed interest in the Neo-Babylonian period both in cuneiform studies and currently in the new excavations at Babylon itself. Surprisingly this period has not been the subject of Schweich Lectures hitherto and it is now almost twenty-five years since my lecture to the Academy on the then recently discovered Babylonian Chronicles which presented major new evidence for this renowned king. Since then that source has been sifted meticulously and, with the more recent publication of legal and economic texts of this reign, merits reconsideration.

The reconstruction of the historical and political background with particular reference to Judah is the subject of Lecture I. A survey of the new sources for a present understanding of ancient Babylon, the great city of Nebuchadnezzar's day, occupies Lecture II. Some of the main literary traditions of the time, especially those of the Old Testament, are examined in Lecture III.

It is hoped that some of the considerations put forward here may contribute to the ongoing discussions of the many issues raised and curtail continued use of some outmoded hypotheses and interpretations.

The Lectures delivered orally on February 24, March 1 and 3, 1983 were extracted from the fuller text given here.

D.J.W.
April 1984

v

CONTENTS

CONTENTS

LIST OF PLATES

At end of text

LIST OF FIGURES

ACKNOWLEDGEMENTS

Plate Ia, V and VI are reproduced by permission of the Trustees of the British Museum. Figures 6 and 10 are adapted from G. Bergamini, *Mesopotamia* 12 (1977), pl. 1. Figure 11a is reproduced by courtesy of Professor W. von Soden, *Ugarit-Forschungen* 3 (1971), 260. Plates II, IV and Fig. 7 were drawn by Keith Talbott for the author. All other illustrations are by the author.

ABBREVIATIONS

AASOR The Annual of the American Schools of Oriental Research
ABL R.F. Harper, *Assyrian & Babylonian Letters* (London, 1892–1914)
AfO Archiv für Orientforschung
AJES American Journal of Economics and Sociology
AHwB W von Soden, *Akkadisches Handwörterbuch* (Wiesbaden, 1965–81)
AKA E.A.W. Budge & L.W. King, *The Annals of the Kings of Assyria* (London, 1902)
ANET J.B. Pritchard, *Ancient Near Eastern Texts relating to the Old Testament* (Princeton, 1969)
An.Or. Analecta Orientalia
An.St. Anatolian Studies
AOAT Alter Orient und Altes Testament
BA Biblical Archaeologist
BASOR Bulletin of the American Schools of Oriental Research
BM Babylonian Inscriptions in the collections of the British Museum
Bi.Or. Bibliotheca Orientalis
BM Tablets/objects in the collections of the British Museum
BRM Babylonian Records in the Library of J. Pierpont Morgan
BSOAS Bulletin of the School of Oriental & African Studies, London
BZ Biblische Zeitschrift
CAD The Assyrian Dictionary of the Oriental Institute of the University of Chicago
CAH The Cambridge Ancient History (Cambridge, 1970–1982)
CT Cuneiform Texts from Babylonian Texts in the collections of the British Museum
EI Eretz Israel
FF Forschungen und Fortschritte
FGrH Die Fragmente der griechischen Historiker (1923–1958)
HUCA Hebrew Union College Annual
IEJ Israel Exploration Journal
ISBE International Standard Bible Encyclopedia I–II (Grand Rapids, 1979–82)
JA Journale Asiatique
JANES Journal of the Ancient Near Eastern Society of Columbia University
JAOS Journal of the American Oriental Society
JBL Journal of Biblical Literature
JCS Journal of Cuneiform Studies
JEA Journal of Egyptian Archaeology
JESHO Journal of Economic and Social History of the Orient
JHS Journal of Hellenic Studies
JNWSL Journal of North-West Semitic Languages
JRAS Journal of the Royal Asiatic Society
JSS Journal of Semitic Studies

K	Tablets in the Kouyunjik collection of the British Museum
KAR	Keilschrifttexte aus Assur religiösen Inhalts
KAV	Keilschrifttexte aus Assur verschiedenen Inhalts
MAOG	Mitteilungen der Altorientalischen Gesellschaft
MDP	Mémoires de la Délegation en Perse
MSL	Materialien zum sumerischen Lexikon
MT	Massoretic Text
MVAG	Mitteilungen der Vorderasiatisch-Aegyptischen Gesellschaft
NBC	Tablets in the Babylonian Collection, Yale University
Or.	Orientalia
OT	Old Testament
PEQ	Quarterly Statement of the Palestine Exploration Fund
PRT	E. Klauber, *Politisch-religiöse Texte aus der Sargonidenzeit* (Leipzig, 1913)
PSBA	Proceedings of the Society of Biblical Archaeology
R	H.C. Rawlinson, *The Cuneiform Inscriptions of Western Asia* (London 1866–1909)
RA	Revue d'assyriolgie et d'archéologie orientale
RB	Revue biblique
R1A	Reallexikon der Assyriologie
SBH	G.A. Reisner, *Sumerisch-babylonische Hymnen nach Thontafeln griechischer Zeit* (Berlin, 1896)
St.Or.	Studia Orientalia (Helsinki)
STT	Sultantepe Tablets
TCL	Textes cunéiformes du Louvre
UE	Ur Excavations
UET	Ur Excavations Texts
UF	Ugarit-Forschungen
UVB	Vorläufiger Bericht über die von dem Deutschen Archäologischen Institut und der Deutschen Orient-Gesellschaft aus Mitteln der Deutschen Forschungsgemeinschaft unternommen Ausgrabungen Uruk-Warka
VAB	Vorderasiatische Bibliothek
VAS	Vorderasiatische Schriftdenkmäler
VAT	Tablets in the collections of the Vorderasiatische Abteilung of the Staatliche Museen, Berlin
VT	Vetus Testamentum
WVDOG	Wissenschaftliche Veröffentlichungen der Deutschen Orient-Gesellschaft
WHJP	World History of the Jewish People (Jerusalem, 1979)
WO	Die Welt des Orients
YNER	Yale Near Eastern Researches
YOS	Yale Oriental Series, Babylonian Texts
YOSR	Yale Oriental Series, Researches
ZA	Zeitschrift für Assyriologie
ZDMG	Zeitschrift der Deutschen Morgenländischen Gesellschaft
ZDPV	Zeitschrift des Deutschen Palästina-Vereins

I

NEBUCHADREZZAR

The name of Nebuchadnezzar stands out in the pages of the Old Testament, and thus in the minds of the many influenced by that ancient collection of books, as the king of Babylon who took the people of Judah from Jerusalem into captivity to his distant and, to them, alien land. The strictly historical allusion to these momentous events in Judean state records preserved in the Biblical books of Kings and Chronicles and the more personal record by the prophet Jeremiah of the final days of Judah, with his theological observations on them, give us but a scant picture of the Babylonian king himself. It rests with the historical introduction of the much discussed Book of Daniel (ch. 1–6) to provide a more intimate tradition about the person and character of the king who took over the widespread territories once held by the all-powerful Assyrian state. The purpose of this first lecture is to examine the largely extra-biblical evidence for Nebuchadrezzar's political career.

Most of the sources for this reign stem from Babylon itself and are subject to the accident of survival of the clay tablets written in the cuneiform script. The evidence from these few extant texts emphasises the loss we suffer from the failure of many genres of texts, notably epics, legends and doubtless histories, to survive. These would have been written on perishable materials in Aramaic which was increasingly the *lingua franca* of Babylonia during this Chaldaean period, as it had been for much of Assyria in the early seventh-century, and would continue to be in Babylonia under the Persian administration.[1] A fragmentary text in Aramaic from Babylonia is dated 728 B.C.[2] and in the middle of the seventh century Assyrian officials in Uruk wrote an ostracon in Aramaic to Assur using Babylonian language characteristics, indicating that Aramaic was currently in use in the southern tribal areas.[3] From Nebuchadrezzar's own

[1] CAH III/I (1982), 240; Millard 1983, 101–8; Tadmor 1982, 449–470; Greenfield 1982, 471–482.

[2] BRM I.22

[3] H. Donner u. W. Röllig, *Kanaanische und Aramaische Inschriften* I (1971), 282–3.

reign Aramaic notes on dated cuneiform texts indicate the presence of scribes writing that script as well as, or even in preference, to cuneiform.[4] This extended to Aramaic inscriptions stamped on bricks including some from Nebuchadrezzar's constructions on the Kasr at Babylon. At least one special stamped brick of Nebuchadrezzar appears to refer to the property concerned (*byt 'ldlny*), and others with brief inscriptions may be instructions for the Aramaic speaking and reading builders.[5] The use of Aramaic on objects and on labels attached to them was a practice already attested in Nineveh, Assur and Tell Halaf.[6] According to the Daniel tradition Aramaic was the dialect in which the court officials and experts addressed Nebuchadrezzar in the second year of his reign (2:4). It is also possible that increased exposure to the Aramaic script during the captivity in Mesopotamia led to the change there, by Jews, to the so-called 'square' Neo-Hebrew script.[7]

The Name

The use of the name Nebuchadrezzar throughout these lectures for the commoner anglicised form Nebuchadnezzar may require explanation. Both occur in the Bible, the more frequent Hebrew נְבוּכַדְנֶאצַּר (*nᵉbûkadne'ṣṣar*)[8] and its LXX counterpart Ναβουχόδὸνοσωρ is usually taken to be a later, and by some corrupt, form of the contemporary Babylonian *Nabû-kudurri-uṣur*. However the writing of the name with *n* is actually attested in an Aramaic tablet dated to Nebuchadrezzar's thirty-fourth year.[9] There is no need then to assume that Nebuchadnezzar

---

[4] Vattioni 1970, Nos. 42, 44, 45, 94, 114–120, 133, 137–141 (from Neirab); McEwan 1982, No. 2. I owe these references to Mr A.R. Millard.

[5] CIS II/I (1889) 56–64 (Nos. 53–62); Berger 1973, 22–3; cf. Koldewey 1914, 80–1, figs. 52–3 160 (*lblhy*); Driver 1976 pl. 17.2 = Walker 1981, 82 (BM. 90136).

[6] Vattioni 1970, 493ff., Nos. 23–4, 26, 143–4, 149–52; Degen 1972, 49–57; Lipiński 1975, 83–142.

[7] Barnett 1982, 5.

[8] MT 61 occurrences with many variants e.g. *Nᵉbûkadne'ṣṣar* with *wāw* in *Nᵉbû*(w) in 2 Kings 24:11; 25:22; Jer. 27:6, 8, 20; 28:3; 29:1, 3; Dan. 1:1, 2 Chron. 36:6, 7, 10, 13; and without it in 2 Kings 24:1, 10; 25:1, 8; Jer. 28:11, 14; 1 Chron. 5:41. The Aramaic of Daniel has *wāw* after the *bēt* 29 times but it is omitted in Dan. 1:18; 2:1; 5:11, 18 as in the Hebrew of Daniel. The almost unanimous LXX *nabouchonosoros* may, have been used by Josephus in referring to Jewish traditions while he used *nabokadrosoros* when quoting from Berossos (Van Selms 1974, 223–4).

[9] Starcky 1960, 100 (B.5); נבוכדנצר On Nebuchadnezzar as an inaccurate form of Nebukadrezzar see Brinkman 1968, 41 and commonly in O.T. commentaries e.g. Porteous 1965, 20, 27.

reflects an Aramaic pronunciation since the shift $r > n$ occurs in other transcriptions of names in Babylonian.[10] In the Old Testament Nebuchadrezzar, the less common Hebrew נְבוּכַדְרֶאצַּר ($n^e bûkadre'ṣṣar$) is used in the books of Jeremiah and Ezekiel.[11] This is a near transliteration of the Babylonian royal name which is likewise written with various syllabic spellings *na-bi-um-ku-du-ur/dur/dúr/-ri/ru-ú/u-ṣu-ùr/ṣur*[12] or, more commonly in Sumerian with logograms (.[Id]ná.níg.du.uri or [d]ná.níg.du.šeš) and this may indicate a closer contact with the name as pronounced.

The meaning of the name formerly given as 'O Nabû, protect the boundary'[13] is now more likely to be interpreted as 'O Nabû, protect my offspring'.[14] The precise meaning of *kudurru* (Assyr. *kadurru*) is not clear,[15] it occurs in association with *aplu*, ('heir') and *šumu* ('name, progeny').[16] There is no reason to believe that any confusion of this word with *kudurru*, 'boundary (line), region' was intentional.[17] Nor is there support for the theory of van Selms that in this particular name *kudurru* was a play on *kūdanu* meaning 'O Nabû, protect the mule' and the name *Nabû-kudurri-uṣur* was thus a nickname originating from the years of unrest during his reign.[18] Apart from the absence of such a practice in Babylonian royal names, the earlier occurence of the name held by a respected ruler is against this. It is to be noted that the element *kudurru* is found in the place normally occupied in personal names by words denoting lineage.[19] The personal name Kudurru served as a name in its own right as well as an abbreviation of names compounded with it.[20] Names of the type *DN-kudurri-uṣur* are well attested from the Middle Babylonian period.[21] At that time Nabû-kudurri-uṣur

---

[10] Berger 1975, 228–30; cf.1 Chron. 3:18.

[11] MT 31 times (the only exception being Jer. 27:6; 29:3). The MT employs eight (insignificantly) variant forms in writing this name.

[12] E.g. Tallqvist 1906, 137.

[13] E.g. Tallqvist 1906, 152.

[14] Brinkman 1968, 104, n. 565.

[15] Cf. Erimhuš V (*TCL* 6 35:34) = bulúg.

[16] MDP 2 pl. 23, vii. 8; King 1912, 6 iii. 40.

[17] *CAD* 8 (1971), 497.

[18] Van Selms 1974, 223–9.

[19] E.g. Nabû–lipi/nipišti/rīhta/šuma/zēra/tali-uṣur (Tallqvist 1906 ad nomem).

[20] Stamm 1939, 43. For Kudurru (níg. du), son of Bēl-kāṣir in Nebuchadrezzar's reign see Strassmaier 1889, 91:11; 26:11; Dougherty 1923, Nos. 11:2; 35:10; 61:3 etc.

[21] Enlil-kudurri-uṣur (III R 4 No. 3: 3–4); Marduk-kudurri-uṣur (MDP 6 pl. 10 iii, 19), Ninurta-kudurri-uṣur (King 1912 16–17 v. 9, 18, 24).

(Nebuchadrezzar I), son of Ninurta-nādin-šumi, was king of Babylon (1124–1103 B.C.) and renowned for his restoration of the statue of Marduk from captivity in Elam and for his revenge on those people for their sack of Babylon.[22] Indeed, it is highly probable that the later Nebuchadrezzar was named after this illustrious royal predecessor, who had claimed legitimacy by reference to the antediluvian rulers as in the Sumerian King List, to the Semitic centre of Sippar, to the dynasties of Nippur and Isin and also to the late Amorite tradition.[23] The name Nebuchadrezzar is otherwise only rarely attested. This appears to have been so also in the second millennium when apart from the one king of that name it is only dubiously attested of a herald (nāgiru) of Nannar.[24] In neo-Assyrian economic texts there are two possible references. One to ^{d}pa.nĭg.du.pap who was a door-keeper who witnessed a transaction in the eponym of Mannu-ki-ahhē.[25] The same individual may be referred to in two other broken contexts.[26] Millard has suggested that the name Nebuchadrezzar given in a Babylonian Chronicle fragment to the otherwise unattested brother of Širiqti-Šuqamunu, who ruled Babylonia for three months about 996 B.C., is an error, or byname, for his predecessor Ninurta-kudurri-uṣur.[27] It is not unreasonable that Nabopolassar, in establishing what has long been customarily considered a new dynasty,[28] but which the Chaldeans themselves may have considered to date from Nabû - nāṣir (746–734 B.C.) a century earlier, should grant this name to his son as the designated heir.[29] It may be questioned whether it was granted as a 'throne name' for, as was the custom, no Babylonian commoner thereafter bore this name.[30] The assumption of the name by one[31] or two[32] usurpers (Nidin-Bēl, Arahu)

[22] Brinkman 1968, 104–110; Wiseman 1975, 455–6.
[23] Lambert 1974, 432–4; Hallo 1971, 146 also implies that the name was held by a previous governor of the Sealand.
[24] King 1912, 6 ii 24 and an unpublished M. Babylonian text from Nippur (113, 157 i:19; ix:12).
[25] Johns 1898, 50:10 (K. 336).
[26] Johns 1898, III 230 = 137 r. 6 restored igi ^{d}nà.nĭg.du.[pap]; K. 710 (III R 52 1 200); ABL 859, 2; cf. ABL 1106: r. 13–4; Brinkman 1977, 312.
[27] Iraq 26 (1964), 30; Brinkman 1968, 164; followed by Grayson 1975, 130.
[28] Olmstead 1925, 29–30.
[29] Langdon 1912, 62, ii 71–iii, 1.
[30] Cf. RlA VI (1980), 150; Wiseman 1980, 154; a full study of throne-names is still required. Against the non-recurrence of a name other than in a ruling family is Šarru-kēn a nāqidu at Uruk in Cyrus 4 (YOS 7 39, 11).
[31] Weisberg 1980, xix–xxvi.
[32] Von Voigtlander 1978, 37–8, 60 ll. 85, 91, 94–5; Wiseman 1981, 567.

in the rebellion against Darius in 522/1 B.C. was presumably to show that they aimed to emulate the actions of both Nebuchadrezzar I and II in freeing Babylonia from Elamite (Persian) domination.

In the year he began reconstruction work on the Etemenanki ziggurat Nabopolassar refers to Nebuchadrezzar as his 'eldest son' (*bukru rēštu*)[33] and the Babylonian Chronicle called him 'the chief son, the crown-prince' (*mārśu rabû mār šarri ša bīt rēdūti*).[34] Nebuchadrezzar always described himself as 'the legitimate/true heir of Nebopolssar'[35] and commonly in his standard brick inscriptions as 'the first (or chief) son' (ibila/ašaredu) or simply as 'son' (dumu) of Nabopolassar.[36]

Ancestry

While the dynasty inaugurated in Babylon by Nebuchadrezzar's father, Nabū-apla-uṣur (Nabopolassar), on November 22/23 626 B.C.[37] is variously called Neo-Babylonian or Chaldean, Hallo considers that 'with equal justice it might be called the Third Dynasty of the Sea-land, or the Dynasty of Bit-Iakin, for although it is impossible to prove Nabopolassar's actual descent from this southernmost and strongest of the Chaldean tribes, his career certainly followed the pattern of earlier members of the house of Iakini'.[38] Presumably he had the career of Marduk-apla-iddina II (the biblical Merodach-baladan) in mind.[39] The traditional view that Nabopolassar was a son of Bēl-ibni and thus a member of the ruling Chaldean tribe Bīt-Yakīn[40] is not supported by any sure evidence. The only connection with the Sea-land rests on a reference in a colophon on a ritual text written three hundred years later in the reign of Seleucus and Antiochus (*Siluku u antiukus*) by a *mašmašu*–priest, Kidin-Anu of Uruk, stating that the original text had been plundered from Uruk by Nabopolassar 'King of the

---

[33] Langdon 1912, 62 ii 72 (possibly to be dated 623–620 B.C.). The phrase is used only of royal princes in the Neo-Babylonian period (CAD 2 (1965), 310 sub *bukru*).

[34] Wiseman 1956, BM. 22047,6); Grayson 1975, 97.

[35] Langdon 1912 96 i 5.

[36] Walker 1981, Nos. 89–102.

[37] Wiseman 1956, 93–4 (BM. 49656, 5–7).

[38] Hallo 1971, 145.

[39] Brinkman 1964, 6–53.

[40] Olmstead 1925, 29–30.

Sea-land' (*šar* ^*māt*^*tamtim*).[41] There is no evidence that
Nabopolassar even had to attack Uruk, let alone plunder it. He
was immediately recognised by the citizens there and in outlying
cities before assuming the throne in Babylon itself.[42] The
evidence of association with the Sea-land is therefore suspect
and does not indicate whether he held the title before or after he
became king of Babylonia.[43] Nor was it a title known to have
been used by him.

Nabopolassar himself claimed to be a native of Babylonia but
to have not been a member of a recognised royal ruling family
(*mār la mammāna*) while a youth (*ina meṣherūtiya*).[44] In his
titulary he never gives his father's name, probably because he
was not of the previous royal line in Babylonia which had been
interrupted for more than a century by Assyrian appointees.
Nabopolassar may have become a ruler (*mlk*) of a tribe[45] who
held sway at Uruk according to a Seleucid copy of a 'prophecy',
composed soon after Nebuchadrezzar came to the throne,
naming him 'King of Uruk'.[46] According to Berossus
Nabopolassar 'had been appointed general by Sarakos (i.e.
Sin-šar-iškun, died 612), the king of the Chaldaeans when
Sarakos marched against Nineveh.'[47] This appears to be a
misrepresentation of the part Nabopolassar played in the attack
on Nineveh in 612 B.C.[48] One late interpretation sees
Nabopolassar in Bupolassaros, cited by Berossus as a general of
Assyrian forces sent by the same Sarakos into southern
Babylonia to subdue an invading army and who later rebelled.[49]
Berossus correctly assigns Nabopolassar a reign of twenty years
reckoning by his full regnal years.[50]

[41] Thureau-Dangin 1921, 65 l. 47.

[42] Wiseman 1956, 93–4 (BM. 49656, 5–7, Sippar); *JNES* 3 (1944) 44. (NCBT 589 & NCBT 557 unpublished).

[43] Von Voigtlander 1964, 17.

[44] Langdon 1912, 66 4, 11 (*ina māti abbanû*). *Mār la mammāna* is distinguished in *RlA* 6 (1980) 152 from *la mammāna*, 'a non-person, non-gentleman' but here it accords with the use in the King Lists of a person not in the normal line of rulers (*JNES* 13 (1954), 214 ii 4, 6, 10 etc.; cf. Lambert 1960, 194 23; *ABL* 521, 6. *meṣherūti* denotes a minor (*Or* 20 (1951), 155), an age definable medically (Köcher 1963 168:72; *AMT* 43 i.2) and when a person could not know whether he had committed a sin (CAD 10/2 (1977), 37 sub *meṣherūtu*).

[45] Cf. Millard 1982, 64 l. 19 where Akkad. *šakin māti* is translated by Aram. *mlk*.

[46] Hunger 1975, 372 ll. 11–15.

[47] Burstein 1978, 26.

[48] Cf. Grayson 1975, 93 28.

[49] Von Voigtlander 1964, 17; Burstein 1978, 26 (6C).

[50] Burstein 1978, 24 (III. 4).

The Old Testament uses 'Chaldean' (*kaśdîm*) for the rulers of Babylon from Nebuchadrezzar onwards in accordance with the normal contemporary reference to the dynasty by outsiders.[51] Two references to possible ancestors of Nebuchadrezzar occur in economic texts. One is to an Ilu-bāni 'father (i.e. ancestor) of Nebuchadrezzar dated to the twentieth year of Nabopolassar (606/5 B.C.),[52] the other to a Ṭābiya 'father of Nebuchadrezzăr' in the fourteenth year of Šamaš-šum-ukin (654 B.C.).[53] If the latter was a reference to our Nebuchadrezzar it might go some way to explain Berossus' assertion that Nebuchadrezzar was 'still in the prime of life' when sent by his father against Egypt and Syria in 605 B.C. However, Berossus may not be reliable here since he interprets events in accordance with Seleucid experience.[54] However, if these texts refer to the same Nebuchadrezzar, they would indicate a possible ancestry going back to Nabû-nāṣir.[55]

Nebuchadrezzar's Family

Nebuchadrezzar had a brother Nabû-šuma-lišir described by his father as 'his next succeeding brother, my favourite small child, the second born' (*talīmšu šerram sīt libbiya duppušu dadua*). Both were present to carry the symbolic basket and hoe when their father inaugurated new work on the ziggurat in Babylon.[56] In Nebuchadrezzar's third year the broken Babylonian Chronicle makes another allusion to this brother Nabû-šuma-lišir.[57] While it is possible to conjecture that this marks the commencement of political difficulties caused by a revolt within the palace, the reference could equally be to the death of this brother but not to both.[58] Both types of events are

---

[51] So Jeremiah (77 times), Ezekiel (15) and the 'Deuteronomist' historian (passim).

[52] Moore 1939, 21:8.

[53] Moore 1939, 12:46.

[54] Burstein 1978, 26 Bl and n. 102.

[55] Moore 1939, 15:6; cf. 12:45.

[56] Langdon 1912, 62 iii 6–11. For *talīmu* as 'next in order' see *Iraq* 20 (1958), 84 n. P. 86; *JANES* 5 (1973), 172; Ahmed 1968, 84 n. 96 argues for 'partner-brother' and *MSL* XII (1963), 85 tam.ma: *talīma* for 'favoured brother'; as AHwB 1310.

[57] Wiseman 1956, 70 (BM. 21946 r.2'–4'). There it is assumed that this describes events in the third year since the next entry is marked 'year 4'.

[58] Von Voigtlander 1964, 106 n. 38 restores ᵈag.mu.si.d[i šeš lugal *ina* tin.tir.ki *i-mu-ut*], but the lacuna is insufficient for this. If death followed illness the restoration could be ᵈag.mu.si.[di šeš lugal GIG-*ma* ÚŠ/nam.meš].

noted elsewhere in the Chronicle.[59] Another son of Nabopolassar, and so brother of Nebuchadrezzar, is Nabû-zēr-ušabši, named in a sale document dated in Nebuchadrezzar's final (43rd) year. It should be noted that one Nabû-ušabši governor of Uruk in 650 B.C. had a brother who was also called Nebuchadrezzar.[60]

There has survived no reference to Nebuchadrezzar's wives in the Babylonian texts. One, Amytis, is named by Berossus who records that 'Nabopolasoros sent troops to the assistance of Astyages, the tribal chieftain and satrap of the Medes in order to obtain a daughter of Astyages, Amyitis, as wife for his son Nabukodrossoros'.[61] Syncellus preserved the name also as Amyitis[62] whereas Ctesias says that Amytis was the name of the daughter of Astyages married to Cyrus I.[63] The former is more likely in that it follows the long standing relations between Babylonia and the Medes established earlier when Nabopolassar made (or re-established) a treaty of 'good will and good relations' (*ṭûbtu u sulummû*)[64] with Umakištar in his twelfth year. This led two years later to the combined sack of Nineveh. The relationship survived at least until a later Babylonian king Labynetus (λαβενετος) mediated between the Medes and Lydia after the R. Halys' battle was terminated by a solar eclipse on 28 May in 585 B.C.[65] The Babylonian king who acted then with the ruler (*syennesis*) of U. Cilicia (Hilakku)[66] could well have been Nebuchadrezzar himself, called upon by the terms of the earlier treaty and marriage settlement to act as a witness, if not mediator, on behalf of his father-in-law. There, however, is no direct evidence that the Babylonian king was a direct party to the settlement.[67] Both the Babylonian and Cilician participants could have been required as witnesses being the overlords of the territories which bordered those of the principal contesting

---

[59] Grayson 1975, 71:11; 86:31; 127:29 cf. 85:22.
[60] Moore 1939, 58:11; ABL 859, 1106 (see Dietrich 1970, 89–96 for references).
[61] Burstein 1978, 25; the Armenian Version of Eusebius names her 'the Amuhean'.
[62] F Gr H 3 CI 680 7d.
[63] Burnstein 1978, 25, n.98 (F Gr H 3 Cl 688 F 9.1).
[64] Wiseman 1982, 313; Wiseman 1956, 58 (BM. 21901, 29); cf. Grayson 1975, 162 (ii 1 and n.); 166, iii 18 ('entente cordiale').
[65] Herodotus I 74.
[66] On Syennesis as a dynastic name see W.F. Albright *BASOR* 120 (1956) 25; Von Voigtlander 1964, 136.
[67] Contra Von Voigtlander 1964, 116–7.

parties. Nebuchadrezzar elsewhere claimed control over Hume and Pirindu (W. Cilicia)[68] and this could have occurred early in his reign, for Que had earlier been an Assyrian province.[69] Herodotus uses the name Labynetos for two kings (I 188) the later of which is usually identified with Nabû-na'id (Nabonidus). Nabonidus was certainly elderly in his ninth regnal year in 547 B.C. at the time of the death of his mother Adad-Guppi' aged 104,[70] but is named in a text of Nebuchadrezzar's eighth year[71] and so could have acted at the negotiations. The suggestion that Labynetos could have been Nergal-šarra-uṣur the predecessor of Nabonidus is unlikely. He was a high military official (*rab mugi*) sent on diplomatic missions as to Jerusalem, while Nebuchadrezzar himself was at Riblah (Jeremiah 39: 3, 5–8, 13)[72] The identification of Labynetus with Neriglissar cannot be sustained even though later as king Neriglissar campaigned in Cilicia in 557 B.C.[73] Whether it was Nebuchadrezzar himself or Nabonidus present after the battle of the eclipse, Herodotus (I. 188), who grants both the name of Labynetus, would be correct, for it is not impossible that if Nebuchadrezzar himself were not present he could have sent Nabonidus as his representative. Hence that official is simply called 'Labynetus of Babylon' without indication of royal status.[74]

Eight of Nebuchadrezzar's children have been identified:

i. *Amēl-Marduk* (lú. ^{d}amar.ud; biblical Evil-Merodach) succeeded his father briefly in 562–560 B.C. (cf. Jer. 52:31).[75] His reign was marred by intrigues, some possibly directed against his father so that Berossus' χαλδαικά stated that 'he governed public affairs in an illegal and improper manner,'[76] and a historical epic may indicate that 'the

[68] Lambert 1965, 10–11.
[69] On the identification of Hume see *BASOR* 120 (1950) 22–5; cf. *JCS* 16 (1962), 51; *Iraq* 20 (1958), 202–8.
[70] Gadd 1958, 50 ii 40–6, iii 5–10; Smith 1924, 112 (BM. 35382 ii 14).
[71] Dougherty 1929, 8.
[72] Cf. Von Voigtlander 1964, 136, n.38; 140–1 n.89.
[73] Wiseman 1956, 74–7; Grayson 1975, 103–4.
[74] Contra Braun 1982, 23.
[75] Sack 1972, 119; Langdon 1912, 276 v 25–26; MDP 10, 96; 14, 60; Nassouhi 1926, 66; VS III, 25 (39th year of Neb.).
[76] Burnstein 1978, 28; Sack 1972, 6–41.

Babylon(ian) speaks bad counsel to Amēl-Marduk'.[77] This led to his assassination by his brother-in-law Neriglissar. The age of Amēl-Marduk at his accession is not known but he could well have been of an age to have been associated earlier with the aging Nebuchadrezzar as heir-apparent or co-regent[78] much as Ashurbanapli's sons had been in Assyria.[79]

ii.   *Eanna-šarra-uṣur* (ᴵe.an.na.lugal.urù) is named as 'a royal prince' (*mār šarri*, a.lugal) among fifteen or more persons each given five sila of barley 'for the sick' (*ana mārṣūtu*) at Uruk in a text dated 25th Iyyar of Nebuchadrezzar's 18th year.[80]

Towards the end of Nebuchadrezzar's reign four other sons are named:

iii.   *Marduk-šuma-uṣur* 'a royal prince' (*mār šarri*) in texts recording the payment of tithes to the Ebabbar(a) temple by his *sepīru* at Sippar in Nebuchadrezzar's 40th and 42nd years. (14.II.42 = 12 May 563) and (7.XII. 40 = 16 Feb 564)[81]

iv.   *Marduk-nādin-ahi*, 'a royal prince' (*mār šarri*) is named in a transaction for the purchase of dates by his servant Sin-mār-šarri-uṣur in Nebuchadrezzar's 41st year.[82]

v.   *Mušezib-Marduk* as *mār šarri*[83] and

vi.   *Marduk-nādin-šumi* *mār šarri* are also named once in a contract of Nebuchadrezzar's 41st year.[84]

The name of one daughter is known:

vii.   Kaššaya (ᶠ*Kaš-ša-a* dumu.mí lugal) is mentioned as possessing blue wool used to make an *ullâku* – garment in Nebuchadrezzar's 31st year.[85] This alone does not justify

[77] Grayson 1975A, 88 (BM. 34113, 5´); see below p 102.

[78] Weisberg 1980, xix, No. 9:17 (29 Aug. 562); The use of this to predate Nebuchadrezzar's death is questionable (Wiseman 1981, 567), as is Sack's argument (Sack 1972, 3) for a corregency (which is otherwise probable) based on texts Nos. 56 (BM.80920 r.3), 79 (BM. 58872, 12–13 but read iti.ab). cf. *BSOAS* 37/2 (1974), 451.

[79] Wiseman 1958, 5–9.

[80] Weisberg 1980 xix, No. 142:19.

[81] Pinches 1902, 434–5; Dandamayev 1982B, 36.

[82] Pinches 1902, 435; Brinkman 1968, 119, n.67; Strassmaier 1889, 382:5.

[83] Strassmaier 1889, 381:2.

[84] Strassmaier 1889, 381.

[85] Joannès 1980, 183 (HE.477:3).

the proposal of Joannès that she was 'sans doubte l'ainée des enfants actuallement connus de Nabuchodonosor II' on the basis that her name occurs in one economic text dated earlier than those in which the other sons occur.[86] She made a dedication to dInnin of Uruk[87] and was married to Nergal-šarra-uṣur (Neriglissar),[88] possibly the same as Nergal-sharezer, the Babylonian noble present at the fall of Jerusalem in 587 B.C. (Jeremiah 39:3).[89] Berossus' *Babyloniaca* describes Neriglisaros as 'his (Evilmerodachus = Amēl-Marduk) sister's husband' who laid the plot which led to Amēl-Marduk's death and his own assumption of the throne in August 560 B.C.[90]

It may well be that Belshazzar (Bēl-šarra-uṣur) of whom it is said in Daniel (5:2) that Nebuchadrezzar was 'his father' was a (grand)son of Nebuchadrezzar.[91] Most commentators dismiss this reference as anachronistic. However, the parentage of Nabû-na'id through his grandparents and Adad-Guppi' and her husband Nabû-balatsu-iqbi is well attested,[92] as is the fact that Nabû-na'id 'entrusted the kingship to him', so appointing Belshazzar to act as co-regent, if not as king, during his ten year absence in central Arabia.[93] Nothing is yet known of Nabonidus' wife, so that it is not impossible that she was another daughter of Nebuchadrezzar[94] who married Nabonidus who was already of high rank (lú.lugal) in Nebuchadrezzar's eighth year.[95] The mother of Nabonidus claims that 'I caused (my son) Nabû-na'id, offspring of my womb, to stand before Nebuchadrezzar son of Nabopolassar and (before) Neriglissar, king of Babylon. Day and night he fulfilled his duties to them and continually did what pleased them. . . .'[96] Against Nabonidus' blood connection

---

[86] Joannès 1980, 184.

[87] Labat 1960, 85, 4–5 (undated text).

[88] Weisberg 1974, 450–2 A.3505 ii. 12´ also names Bēl-šuma-iškun, son of Nabû-epir-lā'a as the father of Neriglissar.

[89] Josephus, *Antiq. Jud.* X 135; Bright 1965, 243.

[90] Burnstein 1978, 28; Brinkman 1966, 203.

[91] On the varied use of *māru* 'son, grandson, descendent' see CAD 10 (1977), 308–16. Similar uses are attested for Aramaic *bar*.

[92] Gadd 1958, 46 i. 2.

[93] Dongherty 1929, 105.111; Smith 1924, 84–8.

[94] Millard 1977, 71–2.

[95] Dougherty 1929, 30–2; Pinches 1902, 436 shows that the second copy of this text was incorrectly read as 'son of the king'.

[96] Gadd 1958, 50 ll. 45–8.

with Nebuchadrezzar it could be argued the later dynastic
chronicles' allusion to him is as of 'the dynasty of Harran'.[97] This
could, however, be but an emphasis referring to his own family
line. These possibilities are included in the reconstruction of
Nebuchadrezzar's family in Fig. 1

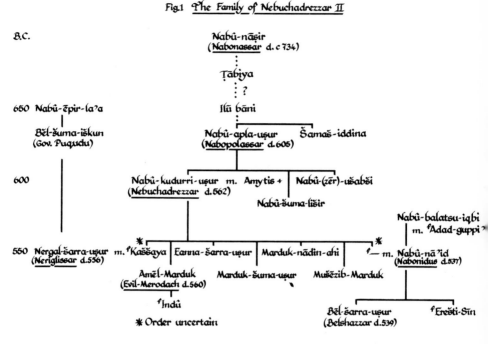

FIG. 1. The Family of Nebuchadrezzar II

Nebuchadrezzar's Career

Apart from the reference to Nebuchadrezzar's attendance at
the ceremony when his father began work on Etemenanki,
probably early in his reign (c. 620 B.C.) little is known of his
youth. He was designated 'crown prince' (mār šarri ša bīt
rēdūti) by 607 B.C. when he called up his own army to march
to mountainous territory, probably East of the Tigris.
Nabopolassar was engaged in field operations in the Harran
area, probably to be dated in 610 B.C., rather than in 616 B.C.[98]
Nebuchadrezzar, if as is generally supposed he was the author of
the letter, raised support for his father from the Eanna

[97] Grayson 1975A 32 ii 12.
[98] Von Voigtlander 1964, 82 n. 14 contra San Nicolò 1941, 41; cf. BM. 21901, 59–61.

authorities in Uruk stating that 'a large force of Medes has gone
to Harran with him.'[99]

Nebuchadrezzar's first major military command after his
father's return to Babylon was to an area, possibly Zamua[100], and
its purpose was to keep control of the mountain tribes on the
border farther south than had been the case in the previous year.
After his father's return from his own month's operations
Nebuchadrezzar occupied the rest of his own personally led
four-month campaign attacking a city, possibly Biranātu, in a
mountainous location, this he set afire and looted after its
capture.[101] Thereafter he appears to have been engaged in
operations over a wide range of the adjacent hills before the
march back to Babylon with the spoil in August (Elul).
Nabopolassar's earlier return was probably for political or
security reasons and to ensure a member of the ruling house
being in the capital. It is unlikely that, as two years later, it was
due to old-age or ill health.[102] In the month following the return
of the crown prince, Nabopolassar called up his army and
marched to Kimuhu, north of Carchemish, (i.e. Assyr.
Kummuh; mod. Samsat, *c.* 38 kms S.E. of Adıyemen).[103] The
capture of this town on the west bank of the Euphrates
threatened the Egyptian lines of communication from Hamath
to Carchemish and is indicative of Nabopolassar's considerable
military skill (Fig. 2).

The importance of Kimuhu as a control-point is endorsed by
the Egyptian reaction to its capture. Following Nabopolassar's
return to Babylon in Shebat (*c.* February 606 B.C.) they
initiated a seige of the Babylonian garrison. The long four
month operation may attest the Egyptian use of near-by
Carchemish as their base. Nabopolassar sought to counter this
move by forming another strong point further south on the
Euphrates at Quramati, protected by three villages (Sunadiri,
Elammu and Dahammu) captured in Ebir-Nāri territory, that is
west of the river. Once again on the Babylonian king's
withdrawal the new garrison was attacked by the Egyptians who
had crossed the Euphrates at Carchemish, which was now firmly

[99] TCL IX 99 (= NBU 324; RA 25 (1925), 27–39.

[100] Reading *Za-[mu-a]* in Wiseman 1956, 64 (BM. 22047, 7); cf. Albright 1956, 29
(*za-[ma-ni]*).

[101] Wiseman 1956, 64 (BM. 22047, 8–11); Grayson 1975, 97.

[102] Berossus apud Josephus *Centra Apionem* I 19 (136).

[103] Wiseman 1956, 64; on the location Albright 1956, 29–30; J.D. Hawkins RlA VI (1983) 339
sub Kummuh.

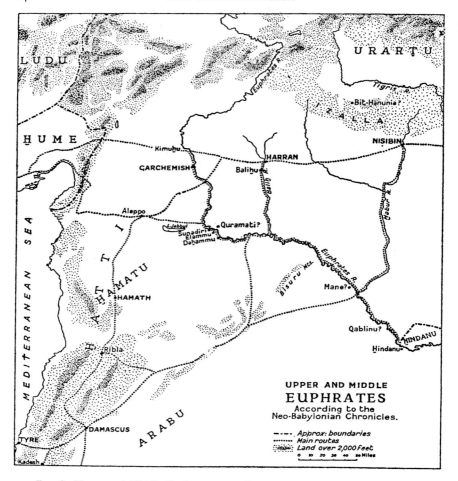

FIG. 2. Upper and Middle Euphrates according to the Neo-Babylonian Chronicles

in their hands. The men from Quramati made a strategic withdrawal southwards.[104]

In 605 B.C., while his father stayed in Babylonia, Nebuchadrezzar is specifically stated to have taken personal control of the army (*pān ummānišu iṣbat*).[105] His objective is stated to be Carchemish and it is likely that the Egyptians had

---

[104] Wiseman 1956, 66–7 (BM. 22047, 24–6).

[105] *ibid* (BM. 21941, 2), cf. r. 6; BM. 21901, 56 and the annals of Ashurbanipal ix. 89 (*mehrit ummanātiya aṣbat*); Tiglath-pileser III Annals ii 75 (*pān quradiya aṣbat*).

themselves by now vacated Quramati for the Babylonians would not have bypassed places held by the enemy or left their line of communication up the R. Euphrates bank exposed. Nebuchadrezzar followed the strategy successfully used by his father against Kimuhu. He crossed to the west bank of the Euphrates to attack the target city, perhaps to gain surprise and cut the Egyptians off from their expected line of retreat. The battle for the city appears to have been closely and fiercely fought until the Egyptians withdrew in seemingly headlong flight. The rout was decisive and Nebuchadrezzar's claim to have 'finished them off completely' (l.5) is justified, for the remnants of the Egyptian army who had managed to escape could not be overtaken until they had reached the district of Hamath. According to the same Babylonian Chronicle 'not a single Egyptian escaped to return home' whereas Josephus, who believed that Nebuchadrezzar's main resolution was to 'fight with Neco, king of Egypt, under whom Syria then was', says they lost ten thousand (i.e. an army) in the battle.[106] The Babylonian Chronicle, as in the case of the Harran conflict in 609 B.C., does not mention the presence of the Egyptian king though other sources indicate it.[107] Berossus wrongly understood the action at Carchemish as punishment of the satrap posted to Egypt, Coele-Syria and Phoenicia who had rebelled.[108]

The victory had an immediate impact on sensitive opinion in the west. Jeremiah forsaw the Babylonians taking control over the whole of the west (25:1–14; 46:1–12) and advocated submission (36:29). The reaction of the opposing military powers is possibly notable for the use of mercenaries on both sides. Following the sack of Nineveh and Harran the Greek states appear to have provided increased help to Egypt and others who sought to stem the Persian advance westwards. Since this mercenary assistance played an important rôle in wars of this reign the evidence for it should be noted. Greek pottery dated to the end of the seventh century B.C. supports the archaeological interpretation of Meṣad Heshavyahu near Ashdod as a Greek mercenary settlement.[109] Woolley argued that the

---

[106] Josephus, *Antiq. Jud.* x vi. 1, cf. *Contra Apionem* I 19.

[107] 2 Kings 23:29f.; Jer. 46:2; 2 Chron. 35:20; cf. BM. 21901, 61.

[108] This error probably stemmed from his treatment of Nebuchadrezzar's western campaigns in the light of Seleucid interests (Burstein 1978, 26 (3.1)).

[109] *IEJ* 14 (1964) 149.

Greek shield decorated with Gorgon's head found at
Carchemish together with fine Egyptian objects and Necho
sealings is evidence of such mercenary presence at the battle of
Carchemish in 605 B.C.[110] He postulates that it had been carried
there by a Greek in Necho's heterogeneous army, perhaps by
one of the Ionians who prompted the offering of spoil from Gaza
to Apollo's temple at Branchidae. The splendour of the shield,
statues and other objects could, however, point to an earlier
dedication in Carchemish which had long been a religious and
trade centre. Their discovery in a large villa on the edge of the
town might simply indicate them to be personal trophies of a
resident for if the rare objects found there are associated it is
unlikely that a mercenary moving up hurriedly from south
Palestine, as did Necho's army to reinforce his garrison, would
take statues with him. The Judean prophet Jeremiah's message
concerning 'the army of pharaoh Necho, king of Egypt, which
was defeated at Carchemish on the River Euphrates by
Nebuchadnezzar King of Babylon' includes a reference to 'men
of Cush and Punt who carry shield and men of Lydia who draw
the bow' (49:1, 9).

On the other side Antimenides, brother of the poet Alcaeus,
fought on behalf of Nebuchadrezzar as a mercenary: 'From the
ends of the earth you are come, with your sword hilt of ivory
bound with gold . . . fighting beside the Babylonians you
accomplished a great labour, and delivered them from distress,
for you slew a warrior who wanted only one palm's breadth of
five royal cubits.'[111] Quinn believes that Antimenides must refer
to the battle fought at Ashkelon in 604 B.C. since a fragmentary
text of Alcaeus refers to that city.[112]

The precise date of the battle of Carchemish can only be set
within limits. The Chronicle states that it occurred within
Nabopolassar's twenty-first year (commencing 12 April 605
B.C.) and before his death (8 Ab = 15/16 August) and time
must be allowed for operations in Syria from which
Nebuchadrezzar was recalled (Plate VI). June–July 605 B.C.
therefore remains the most likely date unless the capture of
Carchemish represents a sudden Blitzkrieg response to the
defeat and retreat of the previous Shebat (January).

[110] Woolley 1921, 128, pl. 28.
[111] Braun 1982, 22 (Alcaeus B.10 translation D. Page).
[112] Quinn 1961, 19–20.

Nebuchadrezzar's troops followed up with the claim to take 'the whole region of Hamath'.[113] It is likely that this area extended as far as Qadesh on the R. Orontes[114] and included Riblah, the town taken by the Egyptians, with Carchemish, in 609 B.C. Riblah, *c.* 35 kms. south-south-west of Homs, was to become the main Babylonian garrison-centre in southern Syria. The site is easily defended and dominates the main route to the Euphrates as well as to the neighbouring forests and valleys which furnished fuel, food and supplies. Riblah was the base for later operations against Jerusalem and remained in use by a garrison until the time of Nabonidus.[115]

Accession

Nebuchadrezzar might have been at Riblah when he heard of his father's death.[116] There is no sure evidence that, at this time, the pursuit had reached the Egyptian border. Josephus' comment that 'the king of Babylon passed over the Euphrates and took all Syria, as far as Pelusium, excepting Judea'[117] may reflect a general survey of the effect of the Babylonian military presence in this and the following few years.

How the news reached Nebuchadrezzar has been a matter of some speculation. In Old Babylonian times fire and smoke signals were used on the Euphrates in the Mari district.[118] In Sargonid Assyria prearranged signals using piles of brushwood (*abru*) transmitted messages as far as Babylon from Assur with the lighted piles set a third of a mile apart.[119] Fire signals were in use in Judah in 588/7.[120] Nevertheless, with the long desert crossing from the R. Euphrates such a system is less likely than the use of a series of fast couriers. Berossus indicates that the news reached Nebuchadrezzar quickly for he 'understood *in a*

---

[113] So correctly Grayson 1975, 99 (BM. 21946, 8) reading ^{KUR} *Ha-[ma-a]-tú ana pat gimrišu ikšu[d]* against Wiseman 1956, 25, 68.

[114] Tell Nebimend (P. Parr, *AfO* 26 (1978–9) 148–9; *Syria* 57 (1980) 29–30); *IEJ* 14 (1964), 272–3.

[115] 2 Kings 25:6, 20–1; Jer. 39: 5–7; 52: 9–27; Cf. Diblat(h) of Ezek. 6:14; BM. 35382:9 (Nabonidus).

[116] Wiseman 1956, 68, 10 (8 Ab = 15 August 605 B.C.).

[117] *Antiq. Jud.* X. 6.

[118] *RA* 35 (1938), 174–86.

[119] Borger 1956, 88:19; Streck 1916, 264 iii 10; Crown 1974, 244–71.

[120] *PEQ* (1982), 107; Jer. 6:1; Zeph. 1:16; 3:18; Lachish Letter 4.

little time that his father Nabopolassar was dead, he set the affairs of Egypt and the other countries in order, and committed the captives he had taken from the Jews and Phoenicians and Syrians, and the nations belonging to Egypt, to some of his friends, that they might conduct that part of the forces that had heavy armour, with the rest of his baggage, to Babylon; whither when he was come, he found the public affairs had been managed by the Chaldaeans, and that the principal person among them had preserved the kingdom for him. Accordingly he now obtained all his father's dominions.'[121] Since Nebuchadrezzar reached Babylon in the month Elul and, presumably on the same day, 'on the first day of Elul (6/7 September 605 B.C.), he sat on the royal throne in Babylon'[122] this tradition may well be right. He had covered the c. 580 miles, assuming a journey from Riblah to Babylon via Ana(tu), in something like twelve to fifteen days. There is no need to assume that the date of ascension was reckoned retrospectively[123] since texts are dated by his reign at Sippar on 24th September[124] and at Babylon six days earlier.[125] The phrase 'to sit on the royal throne' is used nowhere in the Babylonian Chronicles other than of the actual taking over of royal responsibilities in person.[126]

Berossus' statement that 'the kingdom had been preserved for him' is insufficient evidence to conclude that it was a priestly faction acting against any claim by Nebuchadrezzar's brother and that 'this is the first mention of possible schism in the new Babylonian state.'[127] Nebuchadrezzar's position must have been acknowledged quickly and peaceably for the next entry in the Chronicle is his (undated) return to Hattu, a geographical designation used in the Babylonian Chronicles to denote what is today approximately Syria-Lebanon. It is given as the general destination of all Nebuchadrezzar's early operations in the West.[128] There he collected vast booty before his return to

---

[121] Josephus, *Contra Apionem* I, 19 (136–8).

[122] Wiseman 1956, 27 (BM. 21946, 10–11), *ina kussî šarrūti ittašab*; Grayson 1975, 15.

[123] as Von Voigtlander 1964, 105, n.28A.

[124] BM. 49524 unpublished.

[125] This is the likely provenance of NBC 4746, *JNES* 3 (1944), 44.

[126] As of Nabopolassar (Wiseman 1956, 50, BM. 25127, 15) and other kings (Grayson 1975, 70–78, i 2, 10, 13, 23, 28, 31; iii 9, 16, 27, 38; iv 1.

[127] Von Voigtlander 1964, 92.

[128] Hattu included terrain as far east as Carchemish (Wiseman 1956, 72 l. 14) but not as far south as Judah (*ibid.* 72 ll. 11–12).

Babylon in Shebat (February 604) of his 'accession year' (MU.SAG) which lasted from his taking the throne to the first month (Nisan) of the following, his 'first', year. It is significant that the celebration of the New Year Festival (*isinnu akītu*) in the month of Nisan is included by the Babylonian Chronicler as the culminating act of his accession year rather than as the first prominent event of the first official year. The latter was apparently considered as commencing at the point in the celebration when the king had 'taken the hand of Bēl Marduk and the son of Bēl to lead them out in the procession.' The celebration of the New Year Festival was not however, a *sine qua non* of kingship.[129] The years in which the Chronicle states that the festival celebrations were omitted were usually those of internal disturbance or external pressures which necessitated the king's absence abroad. The celebration in Nebuchadrezzar's accession year may well be an indication of his acceptance by the people and of the peaceful conditions which prevailed.

Coronation

While no details are extant of any coronation ceremony for Nebuchadrezzar himself it is likely that the reference to the act of his sitting on the throne implies this as the normal process of succession. Only in the case of usurpers or palace coups is it stated in Assyrian or Babylonian texts that 'they *caused X to sit on the throne*'.[130] Fortunately some details of Nabopolassar's own coronation survive in a broken text[131] and it is likely that some of the features recurred in the ceremony applied to Nebuchadrezzar himself. His father's 'commencement of reign' (*rēš šarrūti*)[132] in Babylon may, however, have included special aspects in that it marked the political independence of Babylonia from Assyria and the popular acclaim which initiated a new 'Chaldean' dynasty. Nonetheless, his ceremony has a number of aspects in common with earlier references to the coronation of

---

[129] Grayson 1975, 35–6.
[130] A legitimate successor claims to have set himself on the throne *(ina kussî šarrūti ittašab)*; *šūšubu* is commonly used of the installation of substitutes (ABL 46:10; 223:16) or of those not normally in line of succession nor otherwise entitled to the throne (Wiseman 1958, 33, 57); Grayson 1975, 77, 23 (Bēl-ibni), 31 (Aššur-nādin-šumi); cf. 159, i 17´.
[131] Grayson 1975 A, 78–86.
[132] Wiseman 1956, 50 (BM. 25127, 15).

the god Marduk,[133] of Ur-Nammu of Ur,[134] a middle-Assyrian king[135], an Urartian ruler[136] and Šamaš-šuma-ukīn of Babylon in 689 B.C.[137] In Nabopolassar's installation the venue seems to have been a palace where 'the princes of the land' (*rubū ša māti*) in assembly made a gesture, apparently voting by raised open fist (*pīta' upnišunu*) declaring that the sovereignty (*šarrūtu*) was his. This was affirmed also by their making the statement that 'the god Bēl, in the assembly of gods has (given) the ruling power (*palû*)' to Nabopolassar. The royal edicts (*pû kīni*) thereafter were accorded this dual popular and divine authority. The divine message continues 'with the *zaqiptu* I will constantly conquer (your) enemies, I will set (your) throne in Babylon (e.ki)'. The ceremonial continued with the throne-official (lú.gu.za.lá") taking the king's hand, presumably to lead him to another location where 'they (the nobles?) put the *zaqiptu* on his head' and then made him sit on the royal throne. The *zaqiptu* placed on his head could be a standard[138] but may well be a specially symbolic crown.[139] That a sceptre was also presented may be deduced from the presence of the sceptre-official (*ša huṭari*)[140] with the chief royal attendant (*ša rēši*), and on the basis of comparison with other enthronment texts. It is not certain whether anointing, as in ancient Israel, was an integral part of the ceremony[141], but this may be expected on similar comparative grounds.

It is noteworthy that it was the nobles, presumably the heads of the leading tribes and families, together with the senior palace officials who were the principal participants in this first part of the ceremony. They invested Nabopolassar with the royal seal and insignia in the inner sanctuary or private rooms *(kummu)* within the palace.[142] It is possible that some part of the more

---

[133] Lambert 1966, 21–2 (ll. 27–30).

[134] *JCS* 20 (1966), 133–41.

[135] Müller 1937, 4–19.

[136] Thureau-Dangin 1912, 50–2 (ii 339–42).

[137] Streck 1916 II, 264–9.

[138] Grayson 1975 A, 85.

[139] Cf. ABL 93, Parpola 1970, 82–3 ll. 12–14 (aga *ina* sag.du *issakan*; P. Calmeyer, '"Personliche Krone" and Diadem', *Archäologische Mitteilungen aus Iran* 9 (1976) 55.

[140] Otherwise attested only as a high neo-Assyrian official (ABL 445:3; PRT 44:8). Cf. RlA VI/I (1980), 149 § 29.

[141] Ben-Barak 1980, 43–56; 1980 A, 66.

[142] Cf. pp. 55–7 and *kummu ellu* in Nebuchadrezzar's own palace (Langdon 1911, 104 ii 3; 136 vii 8).

public ceremony took place in the Nabû ša-harē temple in Babylon.[143]

The ritual continued with the state-officials (*rabûti mat akkadi*[ki])[144] approaching the *kummu* then withdrawing, and perhaps bowing down kissing the ground in front of the king before they did so.[145] In their joy they then exclaimed 'O Lord, O King, may you live forever! May you conquer the land of [your] enemies!' There followed the invocation of the blessing of the gods, beginning with Marduk and Nabû, that the king's days might be long. Even if a number of these ascriptions and acts are best explained as peculiar to Nabopolassar's situation, any accession ceremony for Nebuchadrezzar would have required assent by nobles and officials and so could well have been similar.

Operations against the West

Following his accession to the throne the Chronicle states that 'Nebuchadrezzar', uniquely using his throne-name here rather than the customary 'King of Babylonia (Akkad)', went back again to the Hattu-land where he remained until the month Shebat when he returned to Babylon to celebrate the full New Year Festival, both actions probably indicating a stable situation in the country. In his accession year, and again in his first, third and fourth years, the main consequence of the march to Hattu is stated to be *šalṭāniš ittallak*. Usually with military backing, this resulted in the recovery of much tribute or spoil. The expression has been translated hitherto variously 'march (about) unopposed',[146] 'march about victoriously'[147] or as 'march about enforcing rule' taking it as a technical military term for certain well defined duties involved in mopping up operations.[148] That it was a general description may be surmised from the fact that in

---

[143] Grayson 1975, III 25 (Cambyses).

[144] *rabâni*; cf. lú.gal.meš *ša mat akkadim* (Unger 1931, 285 iv 20); Jer. 39:13 *kôl rabbē melek bābbel*; Kinnier Wilson 1972, 14, 80 'emirs of Babylonia'.

[145] Restoring *it-taš-q[u qaqqaru]* rather than Grayson (1975A, 84 15) *it-taš-b[u-'-ma]*, 'they sat down before him and . . .'

[146] Wiseman 1956, 60, 59; 68 13, 16, 23, r. 5; Albright 1956, 31.

[147] Grayson 1975 ad loc.

[148] Von Voigtlander 1964, 85 n. 49 (but the example given of Jer. 52:12, 27 is inapplicable as it was not a repeated action).

the Nebuchadrezzar Chronicle the target of specifically military operations such as seiges is named. The action of *atalluku* (cf. Heb. *hithallek*) is used either literally or descriptively of a way of life[149] and is associated with the exercise of justice in the description of earlier reigns.[150] The consequences of the action can be dire both in the death-sentence passed on opponents and in the tribute exacted.[151] It follows the subjugation of conquered territory (as after the fall of Nineveh and Assyria, and the battle of Carchemish) as it did the conquest by Sargon II of Ursa's capital of Ulhi of which he says 'I entered like a lord and *šalṭiš attallak* in the palace which was his royal dwelling.'[152] In the light of this Nebuchadrezzar would have located himself at a suitable centre, such as Riblah, from which he directed operations as the supreme overlord both for the collection of tribute and dispensation of justice as he did for example later against the rebel Zedekiah. (Jer. 52: 10–11).[153] Such a sense of Nebuchadrezzar's mission as 'king of justice' is reflected in his Wadi Brissa inscription which maintains that in Hattu he was collecting wood of Lebanon for the temples of Marduk and Nabû, opposing a hostile foreign king who was robbing the region of its riches, reuniting scattered fugitive peoples and making the whole land happy.[154] The literary text which describes Nebuchadrezzar as the just king (*šar mēšarim*), though centring on this rôle within the homeland, ends with a list of the lands from Egypt to Lydia in the West where he was triumphant.[155] It is not without significance that Nebuchadrezzar uses the phrase *ša ina tukulti 'Nabû u [ᵈMar]duk bēlēšu ittallaku* to describe himself on votive offerings.[156]

In his first full year, following a six-month period of exercising control in Hattu (*šalṭāniš ittallaku*), Nebuchadrezzar

---

[149] CAD I 325–6 sub *atalluku*; Wiseman 1980, 155 n. 11.

[150] Cf. *mēšeriš ittallakuma* (Aššur-nāṣir-apli II, AKA 261; 22; 385, iii 128); *mēšeriš ultallituma* (Tiglathpileser I, AKA 63 iv 47); *mēšeriš šalṭiš lu attallak* (Shalmaneser III, 3 R 7 ii 7; *Iraq* 25 (1963), 56 46.

[151] Borger 1956 A iv 61; cf. 104 ii 1; 46 ii 27 (*ultu ṣīt šamši adi ereb šamši šalṭiš attallakuma māhira ūl išī*).

[152] Thureau-Dangin 1912, 34 (P. 216 restored from KAH II, 141).; cf. *šalṭāniš ittallaku ina ālāmi ša* ᵐᵃᵗ*meluhhe* in BM. 41581:16 (unpublished: Antiochus).

[153] Wiseman 1956, 68 13.

[154] Weisbach 1906, 32 ix 13–32; *ANET* (1950), 307.

[155] Lambert 1965, 11.

[156] Nassouhi 1926, 65; *MDP* VI, 56 (Susa); Langdon 1912, 206 and cf. royal epithets with *ittanallaku* (Berger 1973, 75 Nos. 51 a–b).

claims that 'all the kings of Hattu came before him and he received their heavy tribute.'[157] Those paying tribute included Jehoikim of Judah who was to remain a vassal for three years (2 Kings 24:1). No direct mention is made of Jerusalem in the Babylonian Chronicle but only of operations against a city, possibly Ashkelon (BM. 21946, 18–20),[158] whose king was captured in Kislev (November/December 604 B.C.). In Judah this same month a fast was called for all including the outlying peoples who had retreated into Jerusalem, a sure token of the concern felt there (Jer. 36:9). There is no reference in the Babylonian Chronicle to any seige of Jerusalem in Nebuchadrezzar's first six years. From Jehoiakim's violent reaction to Jeremiah's warnings passed to him by his council of ministers, it is apparent that Jerusalem had not yet given in to the Babylonians.[159] The statement in Daniel (1:1) that Nebuchadnezzar, king of Babylon, came to Jerusalem and *wayyaṣar 'aleyha* (RSV 'and beseiged it') could refer to this time. The phrase may mean no more than 'showed hostility' or 'treated as an enemy' and can denote action preliminary to, but not necessarily an actual seige (2 Kings 24:10–11).[160] Daniel 1:1 does not say that Jerusalem was actually taken or that Jehoiakim was taken prisoner. The articles from Yahweh's temple later carried off to the treasure house of the Babylon temple would be included in the general statement of collection of tribute in the Babylonian Chronicle for this year (l. 17). The 'third year of Jehoiakim' of the biblical historian could be a justifiable dating if this covered the twelve months ending in 604 B.C. (Dan 1:1 cf. Jer 46:2).[161]

Jehoiakim himself may well have been treated harshly as a protégé of the Egyptian pharaoh Necho II (2 Kings 23:24, 35) and forced to go to pay tribute to the Babylonians. When Nebuchadrezzar had gained control of the area he allowed Jehoiakim to reinforce the southern border immediately and

---

[157] Wiseman 1956, 68 17; Grayson 1975, 100 15–20.

[158] The restoration ᵘʳᵘ[iš-qi-'i-il-lu-nu] was based on a comparison with iš-qil-lu-na-a in Weidner 1939, 928. The reading remains however uncertain (Grayson 1975, 100 (5:18); *AfO* 22 (1980), 161).

[159] Malamat 1968, 141.

[160] Cf. Deut. 20:12; 2 Kings 16:5; Ct. 8:9; Ps. 139:5.

[161] Jer. 46:2 might refer back to Necho 'who had been defeated at Carchemish', and the dates given could be a separate statement of the date of the message 'in the fourth year of Jehoiakim'.

thereafter 'the king of Egypt did not march out of his country again, because the king of Babylon had taken all his territory, from the Wadi of Egypt to the Euphrates River' (2 Kings 24:7). There is some external evidence which may indicate the Egyptian withdrawal at this time. The Arad excavations and inscriptions show that that frontier fortress, previously destroyed by the Egyptians in 609 B.C. (Stratum VII), was rebuilt *c.* 604 (Stratum VI). The interruption of supplies of wine and oil to the Greek mercenaries (? *lktym*) from a high Judean official Eliashib can be assigned to this same period.[162] If, as is generally thought, the Greek mercenaries at Meṣad Hashavyahu had been under Egyptian control then they may have changed sides since they now appear to be under a Jewish(?) governor.[163] About this time also Antimenides the brother of Alcaeus of Mytilene who had fought for the Babylonians at Ashkelon was welcomed home as a hero.

These operations raise the question of the date of the deportation of Daniel and his companions to Babylon. While this might well have been with the temple vessels taken from Jehoiakim in 604 B.C. it is not impossible that they were taken in the annual exercise by Nebuchadrezzar of emphasizing his overlordship by exacting regular tribute (*šalṭāniš ittallaku*) undertaken in the following three years. The Chronicle for Nebuchadrezzar's third year (602/1 B.C.) especially notes that vast booty, including personnel, was bought from Hattu to Babylonia and this may have been the occasion of their deportation.[164] However, the evidence of Daniel (2:1, 16) weighs in favour of the first or second year. (604/3 B.C.).

By his second year (603/2 B.C.) Nebuchadrezzar was facing such stiff resistance from some point in the west that he had to organise a more powerful military force (*ummānisu kabittu ikṣur*).[165] Although the destination is lost in a lacuna in the broken Chronicle for the year it is assumed that it was once again Hattu, the objective of the previous year as it was to be in the next. The special target was a place, the name of which is now lost, against which Nebuchadrezzar laid seige (*ana muhhi āl[x...] iddi*) by bringing seige towers across mountains.[166] The

[162] Aharoni 1981, 149; cf. Braun 1982, 22.
[163] *IEJ* 12 (1962), 89f.; 10 (1960), 129f; 14 (1964), 148, 158f.; *BASOR* 176 (1964) 29–38.
[164] Wiseman 1977, 335 (on BM. 21946 r. 4).
[165] Wiseman 1956, 70 r. 8, 21.
[166] Grayson 1975, 100 22; 73; *CAD* 11 (1980), 18.

length and outcome of the seige is lost in the lacuna.[167] While it is not impossible that here, or in the gap which follows, there could be some reference to the seige of Jerusalem which led to the arrest and temporary removal of Jehoiakim from Jerusalem,[168] this is unlikely as is the idea that such heavy equipment was used against Ashdod, Ekron or Gaza.[169] The strategic situation was such that the Babylonians as yet made no more than forays from southern Syria. This has hitherto appeared to be contradicted by the interpretation of a letter written on papyrus from a ruler Adon to his overlord in Egypt, found at Saqqara in which he states that what "[I have written to the Lord of Kings is to inform him that the forces] of the King of Babylon have come [and] reach(ed) Aphek . . . [. . .] they have have seized [. . .] for the Lord of Kings pharaoh knows that [your] servant [asks him to send a force to rescue [me]. Do not abandon [me, for your servant did not violate the treaty of the Lord of Kings] and your servant preserved his good relations. And as for this commander [. . .] a governor in the land. And as for the letter of Sindur[. . .]"[170] While there is virtual agreement on the general dating of the letter to the end of the seventh century the identity of the city threatened is much disputed. Several scholars have followed the suggestion made in my first edition of this Babylonian Chronicle that it could be linked with the siege of Ashkelon 12 miles north of Gaza in 604 B.C.[171] This is, I now think, unlikely, since Aga' king of Ashkelon was held in Babylon about this time by Nebuchadrezzar.[172]

Porten has rightly stressed that any link with this letter must depend on the identification of the Aphek (Afek) in it. The location of Adon's city has been variously argued as Gaza,[173]

---

[167] Grayson 1975, 23 follows my original restoration of *šaltāniš ittallak*. This is by no means certain as its use would imply that throughout the seige operation this action was being carried out concurrently. Elsewhere the phrase occurs of action taken alone during a campaign. The lacuna may have contained a reference to the length of the seige [*ultu* ⁱᵗⁱ . . *adi* ⁱᵗⁱ . . *ina muhhi* ᵘʳᵘ . . . . . *iddi*].

[168] 2 Chron. 36:6 cf. Dan. 1:1; Vogt 1957, 90; Malamat 1968, 142.

[169] Rainey 1975, 54–5; Malamat 1975, 131.

[170] Porten 1981, 36; cf. Porten 1980, 39–43 (for physical aspects of Aramaic letters).

[171] Wiseman 1956, 28; Albright 1956, 31 n. 14; *BA* 19 (1956), 55 n. 6 (Friedman); Malamat 1956, 28; Voght 1957, 87–8; Nötscher 1957, 11.

[172] Weidner 1939, 928.

[173] Vogt 1957, 87–8; *ZDPV* 79 (1963), 149 (K. Galling); Malamat 1968, 142–3, n. 11; Freedy & Redford 1970, 477 n.77.

Lachish,[174] Ashdod,[175] or 'Gaza, Ekron or Ashdod',[176] Gaza is
unlikely as it had been under an Egyptian governor and not an
independent king. Gath is not mentioned in contemporary
documents after its destruction by Uzziah (2 Chron 26:6) and
Ashdod had been sacked earlier by both Assyrians and
Egyptians (cf. Jer 25:20). Porten has argued for Ekron itself as
the Philistinian city closest to Aphek-Antipatris.[177] Nevertheless
some seek for a location further north either somewhere on the
Phoenician coast or more specifically at Byblos,[178] Sidon or
possibly Tyre.[179] The readings (and identification of Afek with
Afqa) may be erroneous, and any argument against the assertion
that the route taken from Riblah in the Beqa' was a difficult
one[180] may be vitiated both by the Chronicle statement (l. 22)
that siege-equipment was 'taken across (mountains)' and by
Nebuchadrezzar's own claim that in Syria he had special roads
cut through the Anti-Lebanon mountains for the collection and
transportation of cedar down to the Orontes. He left his 'victory'
stelae carved in archaic and neo-babylonian cuneiform in the
rock faces overlooking the mouth of the R. Litani north of
Tyre.[181] His stated opponent, 'the hostile foreign king' (*šarru
nakru ahu*) who controlled this area and robbed it of its riches,[182]
is usually understood to be a Phoenician king, presumably that
of Tyre and Sidon, but could as well be the Egyptian king
supporting these coastal cities in Phoenicia.

That the siege of Sidon could be the subject of the text
missing in the Babylonian Chronicle (BM. 21946.24' −r.1') is
not impossible. It is unlikely that in the military operations
further south in the following few years the Babylonians would
have left a powerful source of interference of their supply lines
from Riblah unchecked. That the reference might be to the
beginning of the seige of Tyre is also possible, and this could

---

[174] Rainey 1975, 55–6; *Tel Aviv* I (1973), 54 n. l. 22 reading [*la-ki-su*] though [*ina muhhi*^{uru} *ha-za-tú*] elsewhere on the same page.

[175] Tadmor 1956, 229 n. 21.

[176] Malamat 1979, 209.

[177] Porten 1981, 41 based on his reading of the Demotic postscripts as '*qrn*.

[178] Horn 1968, 29f.; Oded 1977, 470; Gibson 1975, 21.

[179] Milik 1967, 561ff.; arguments against this are summarised by Porten 1981, 41.

[180] Horn 1968, 35–6.

[181] Sheriffs 1976, 239 interprets these as following traditional Assyrian imperial theology, but this does not diminish the testimony of their location.

[182] Weissbach 1906, 32 ix 23.

then explain why Tyre appears to have remained neutral when Jehoiakim failed to pay tribute to Babylon in 601 B.C.[183] The loyalty oath sworn by Jehoiakim to Nebuchadrezzar, and presumably by the rulers of the Syrian territories more immediately overrun, was that 'he would surely keep the country for him and attempt no uprising nor show friendliness to the Egyptians'.[184] Tyre may not have been among the Hattu-kings who had paid tribute in 604 B.C., for official representatives (ṣīr)[185] of Tyre and Sidon came to Jerusalem at the beginning of Zedekiah's reign (594/3) as part of the international congress of anti-Babylonian rebels (Jer 27:3). Katzenstein has suggested that Tyre's association with Judah at this time may have been due to a desire for trade contacts through the Negeb now put under Edomic control by Nebuchadrezzar (cf. Jer. 13:19).[186] Certainly mariners of Tyre are listed as present in Babylon in 592 B.C. presumably having been taken from a subjugated city as had been other captives there.[187]

The dating of the major seige of Tyre usually rests on Menander Ephesius: 'Nebuchadnezzar beseiged Tyre for thirteen years in the time of Ithobal the king; after him reigned Baal, ten years.'[188] Though the precise dates for the reign of Ethbaal III of Tyre are disputed,[189] these are currently taken to be 591/0–573/2 B.C. Since Josephus says that 'in the seventh year of the reign of Nebuchadnezzar, he began to beseige Tyre'[190] it has been argued that the commencement of the seige of Tyre would be 598/7, the silence of the Chronicle would then have to be explained as due to its concern with the major attack on Jerusalem in that same year. Failing this the seige is often dated to c. 588/7–573 B.C., the *terminus ad quem* then falling in the reign of Ba'al II (573/2–564/3 B.C.). This would then coincide with the Babylonian domination of the period usually attributed to the rule by 'judges'. In Nebuchadrezzar's fortieth

[183] Cf. Wiseman 1956, 70–1; Josephus *Antiq. Jud.* X 88.

[184] Josephus, *Antiq. Jud.* X 102.

[185] Wiseman 1982, 316.

[186] Katzenstein 1973, 316.

[187] Weidner 1939, 929.

[188] In Josephus, *Contra Apionem* I 21; Philostratus ('History of India' = Judea ?) quoted in Josephus, *Antiq. Jud.* XI 1; X 228.8.

[189] E.g. Eissfeldt 1933, 421–2.

[190] *Contra Apionem* I 21; Von Voigtlander 1964, 134 n.23 proposes a reading of '17th' for '7th' year. Katzenstein 1973, 328 takes this as the 7th year (of Ithobaal) i.e. 585 B.C.

year a Babylonian text dated at Ṣurru (Tyre) implies the control
of Tyre by Milki-eṭēri, governor (*bēl pīhāti*) of the province of
Qadesh.[191] The Babylonian administration was firmly established at Tyre in the following year when a *šandabakku*-official
is mentioned. By 564 Nebuchadrezzar himself was at Tyre for a
text dated there says that 'the king and the men who were with
him went to Tyre',[193] some supplied with warm clothing and
sīru-garments from Erech.[194] The paucity of Neo-Babylonian
texts dated at Tyre, as of those dated at Qadesh further inland,
may of itself not be indicative of the date of the seige. Since the
names of rulers of Tyre *c.* 660–591 B.C. are not known it is not
impossible that another ruler bearing the throne name Ethbaal
lies behind the Menander tradition. The thirteen years of seige
could have been a long blockade requiring annual replacement
of the attacking troops rather than continuous assault. It would
have involved the same techniques, experience, and even
materials as later deployed against Jerusalem. In favour of an
earlier date for a seige *c.* 603–590 would be the rôle of the
Babylonians in Que (Cilicia), already in their hands by 585 B.C.
It could be suggested that, like Assyrian predecessors, the
Babylonians would have hesitated to attempt to penetrate Egypt
as they did in 601, and later in 568/7, without at least closely
containing the cities of Tyre and Sidon whose fleets supported
Babylon's major enemy. There is no sure extra-biblical evidence
of any Babylonian military activity in 'Philistia', the coastal
plain, or in Judah before Nebuchadrezzar's seventh year.

Even if the suggestion that the seige of Tyre began following
that of Sidon in 602 B.C., rather than in the seventh year of
Ethbaal III, that is in *c.* 586/5, is rejected, an earlier occupation
of the mainland opposite Tyre would be expected.[195] This would
then require the restoration of 'against Tyre' in the lacuna of the
Babylonian Chronicle.[196] The seige was an arduous task reflected

[191] BM. 40546 dated 22 Tammuz, 40th. year Neb. (= 12 July 565); cf. *IEJ* 14 (1964), 272–3;
Pinches 1902, 401; McEwan 1982, 5 n.2.

[192] Dougherty 1923, No. 94 (8.v.41 Neb. = 8 August 564 B.C.); pp. 4–5; Unger 1926, 314–7.
McEwan 1982, 5 is a sale contract for the purchase of a female slave by a man from Nippur,
presumably on active service at Tyre and dated 24. iv. 41 Neb.

[193] Dougherty 1923, 23 No. 151.

[194] Dougherty 1933, 135:5 (12.1.42 Neb. = 10 Apr. 563 B.C.).

[195] Katzenstein 1973, 324–31.

[196] BM. 21946, 22 (Wiseman 1956, 70) should then be restored [*ina* ugu^uru *Ṣu-ru iddi ṣapāti
rabûti ušbal[kit]*. *šubalkutu* is used of crossing mountains (*Iraq* 20 (1958), 183, No. 39:60;
Ar.Or. 17 (1949), 204:18).

in Ezekiel's later prophecy dated in 571 (29:17–18).[197] The king of Tyre who headed the list of the procession of kings in Babylon about 570. B.C. could have been Ethbaal III. If so his successor at Tyre would then have been a client-ruler with a Babylonian appointed official watching over him, a process repeated during the subsequent rule of 'judges' there.[198]

Having established his control over Syria and with vassal kings in office in southern Palestine Nebuchadrezzar, according to his Chronicle, began his fourth year with further law enforcement operations in Hattu. The work could have included the annual reinforcement and replacement of Babylonian garrisons stationed there to support the Babylonian nominees whose rôle included the provision of supplies and of intelligence to Babylon.[199] The latter must have alerted Nebuchadrezzar to take personal command of his army in Kislev (Nov/Dec. 601 B.C. *pān ummānišu iṣbat*) with the stated objective of a march to Egypt. The time-scale of the operation precludes this advance being the occasion of Adon's appeal to Egypt for help.[200] The Egyptian reaction was for the Saite king Necho II to call out his own army. The consequent clash of the major military forces of the day is described dramatically: 'In an open battle they smote each other and inflicted a major defeat on each other.'[201] The action was hard-fought, the Egyptian vigour being in part due to their re-equipment with additional mercenaries since their defeat at Carchemish and to their restraint in not getting involved, beyond garrisoning the southern Palestinian border, meanwhile. The Babylonian losses were such as to require a year's respite from military operations specifically devoted to re-equipment of the army with chariots and horses. These presumably had suffered the most in the open battle. Since Josephus summarises the Babylonian early conquests in the west as 'as far as Pelusium' it may be assumed that the contestants met in this region, possibly at Magdalus. The Egyptians may by now have penetrated as far as Gaza.[202]

Although this battle effectively ended any Saite control in

[197] i.e. 26 April 571 B.C.; *JBL* 69 (1950), 65.
[198] Katzenstein 1973, 332; Josephus, *Contra Apionem* I 157 contra Saggs 1962, 143.
[199] Wiseman 1980, 147–9; *JNES* 30 (1971), 186–217; *HUCA* 50 (1979), 1–15.
[200] Contra Malamat 1968, 143.
[201] Wiseman 1956, 70 (BM. 21946, r. 6–7); Grayson 1975, 101.
[202] *Antiq. Jud.* X 6 86; Lipiński 1972, 236; Katzenstein 1983, 251.

Asia by land, Jehoiakim's change of allegiance from Babylon to Egypt after this battle presumably indicates that he, at least, thought the Egyptians to be, and likely to be, the stronger party in southern Palestine. Nevertheless neither Necho II nor Psammetichus II faced direct confrontation with the Babylonians thereafter though maintaining naval contact with the Phoenician coastal cities (Kharu) with a visit to Byblos in 591 B.C.[203] In the days of their successor Apries, the Egyptians showed a marked restraint when Zedekiah called for help at the time of the major and final attack on Judah in 588/7. Then they retreated before contact was a possibility, leaving Jerusalem to be sacked.[204] The intention of Nebuchadrezzar's initiative was to take Egyptian pressure off the Babylonian garrisons in Syro-Palestine during a period of consolidation of control. In this he was to a large measure successful. There is no evidence to show that the aim was an invasion of Egypt[205] so much as a curtailment of Egyptian influence on the cities of the *via maris* and hinterland.

Following the period devoted to refurbishing his army (early 600–October 599 B.C.) Nebuchadrezzar's personal presence was once more needed in Hattu-land from which he directed raiding parties against the Arabs in the desert borders of southern and central Syria.[206] For this purpose Carchemish, Hamath and Riblah would have served well as centres. The traditional method of plundering and firing Arab camps, depriving them of domestic animals (*bulu*) and capturing their gods, as developed by the Assyrians,[207] would have been sufficient to protect the main Babylonian routes to Riblah including that via Tadmor. The action would have brought the Babylonians closer to Judah if, as is commonly now accepted, the target was 'Qedar and the kingdoms of Hazor (or *hsr*) which Nebuchadrezzar king of Babylon smote' according to Jeremiah's

---

[203] *VT* 1 (1951), 142; Drioton 1952, 583–4, 594; Spalinger 1977, 232.

[204] Kitchen 1973, 407; Jer. 37:5; Josephus, *Antiq.* Jud. X 108–111; The 'petition of Patêsi' dated to the ninth year of Darius I (512 B.C.) refers back to this; cf. *ZAW* 30 (1910), 288.

[205] Contra Spalinger 1977, 231.

[206] Wiseman 1956, 70 (BM. 21946, r. 10 & n.1); cf. Grayson 1975, 101 n. 10. The determinative kur before *arabi* is uncertain and the reading lú more likely in that in this Chronicle *mādūtu* refers more commonly to people than things.

[207] *Iraq* 16 (1954), 179–81; Borger 1956, iv 2–29.

oracle. (49:28–33).[208] It would be at this time, or in the following year, that Nebuchadrezzar had the opportunity of imposing the requirement, or simply stimulating the opportunity, for raiding the border of rebel Judah (2 Kings 24:2).[209] The raiders are named as Arameans, Moabites and Ammonites by the Deuteronomist historian (2 Kings 24:2). It has been supposed that the first should read 'bands of Edomites' on the basis of Jer. 35:11 and the Peshitta at both references.[210] However, the location of the starting-point of the current Babylonian operations in north and central Syria at this time, as well as two years later, is against this.[211] Also there is the tradition preserved in Judith (2:23–27) which tells how the Babylonian general 'plundered all the people of Rassis and the Ishmaelites who lived along the desert, south of the country of the Chelleans. . . . He surrounded all the Midianites and burned their tents and plundered their sheepfolds. Then he went down into the plain of Damascus during the wheat harvest and burned all their fields and destroyed their flocks and herds, sacked their cities, ravaged their lands and put to death all their young men with the edge of the sword.' Greenfield has suggested that the details are based on the Babylonian Chronicle[212] and that the Chelleans be identified with χαλον ποταμόν of Xenophon[213] and the northern border of the Syrian desert along the al-Quweiq river outside Aleppo.[214] This could explain the references to 'Aramaeans' since this was close to their traditional tribal lands. The activities of the Edomites further south on the border of Judah at this time may be reflected in Arad Letter No. 24. This would be in keeping with their usual practice (Zeph 2:8; Jer 49:1).[215] Strong evidence for the correctness of the 'Aram' tradition in 2 Kings 24:12 is the use of *Aramu*, with *Kaldu* and *Hattu* in a late Babylonian tribute list.[216]

---

[208] Wiseman 1956, 31–2 and n.3; Malamat 1956, 254–6; Vogt 1957, 92; Dumbrell 1972, 99–109; Gadd 1958, 78.

[209] Malamat 1968, 143.

[210] Eph'al 1982, 1973 n. 587.

[211] Bartlett 1982, 16.

[212] *Yediot* 28 (1964), 204–8; cf. J. Lewy, *ZDMG* 81 (1927), LII–LIX.

[213] *Anabasis* I 4.

[214] References in Eph'al 1982, 173–4 n. 591.

[215] Aharoni 1981, 46–9; *BA* 31 (1968), 17f.; A. Lemaire, 'L'ostrocon "Ramat-Negeb" et la topographie historique de Négeb', *Semitica* 23 (1973), 11–26.

[216] Wiseman 1967, 495 ii 13', iii. 9.

The Capture of Jerusalem

Nebuchadrezzar was himself much occupied in Babylon until Kislev of his seventh year (Dec/Jan 598/7) when Hattu was once more the destination of his remustered army. From there, again probably Riblah, he sent his forces to lay seige on Jerusalem, 'he encamped against the City of Judah (āl Yahudu) and on the second day of the month Adar he captured the city (and) seized the king. He appointed in it a king of his own choice (heart) and taking heavy tribute brought it back into Babylon' (Plate VI).[217] There may have been insufficient time for the operation to have been a reaction to the death of Jehoiakim which occurred but a month before the army left Babylon (2 Chron. 36:9).[218] Although the operations in the West are initially to Hattu, Jerusalem was a specific target, chosen in response to the three-year long rebellion by Judah. It had been curbed only partially by the incursions of raiders from neighbouring territories, spurred on by Babylonian encouragement.

That a specific date for the capture of Jerusalem is given (15/16 March 597 B.C.) shows its importance in Babylonian eyes. The Chronicle had given a precise date for the taking of the lesser towns of Rahilu and Ruggulitu,[219] but only elsewhere, in this Chronicle, for the death of Nabopolassar and for Nebuchadrezzar's accession to the throne. The date may have been given also to mark the accession of Mattaniah – Zedekiah (2 Kings 24:17; Jer 37:1)[220] or to emphasise that the seige was of only a short duration.[221] The latter may have followed from Nebuchadrezzar joining the beseiging troops (2 Kings 24:11), for his presence would have stimulated the desire of the peace faction among the defenders to give in.

The arrangement to select, collect and transport the skilled prisoners and the valuable booty (bilasa kabittu) which had been captured would have taken a few weeks and is elsewhere dated to 'when the year had turned' (2 Chron. 36:10) i.e. to the

---

[217] Wiseman 1956, 72; Grayson 1975, 102 (BM. 21946, r. 11´–13´ reading itērib (or ultērib 'sent back') for TU.i[b].

[218] Contra Noth 1958, 137–9.

[219] Grayson 1975, 93, 95 (BM. 21901, 33, 57).

[220] There is no certainty that Zedekiah was a 'throne-name' since these were not given to vassals outside Babylonia. Cf. p. 4 n.30.

[221] Malamat 1968, 144 ('no more than a month').

month Nisan (cf. Ezek. 40:1) which marked the beginning of the eighth year of Nebuchadrezzar's reign (2 Kings 24:12).[222] By this time Nebuchadrezzar had returned to his own capital to which he had had Jehoiachin taken and the Jerusalem temple vessels had been dedicated in the temple of Marduk there (2 Chron. 36:10; Dan 1:1; 5:2).[223] Jehoiachin's successor Zedekiah was installed before the departure of Nebuchadrezzar, three months and ten days after Jehoiakim's death (6/7 December 598 B.C.) – and therefore before the fall of the city, implying that he was outside it at the time. That Zedekiah was set up as ruler after the actual departure of Jehoiachin requires the assumption that a Tishri new year calendar reckoning was used, as does Malamat.[224] The majority of scholars, however, still opt for the Nisan calendar.[225] On installation Nebuchadrezzar made Zedekiah swear an oath by Yahweh his own deity. The western practise being for such oaths to be in the name of the god(s) of the subordinated state, supplementing the name of the principal god of the sovereign power.[226] The precise form of loyalty-oath would have been a local variant to that used earlier by Assyrian kings,[227] with specific clauses the breaking of which would justify, as they were to ten years later, further action by the overlord. (Jer 39:5–7)

Certainly in the month Tebet of his following year (January 596) Nebuchadrezzar is once more stated to have gone to Hattu as far as Carchemish and, in the following month, to have returned to his own land.[228] The small breaks in the text are insufficient to warrant any major detail having been lost, perhaps only the place from which he started his return home.[229] It is not impossible that once again Nebuchadrezzar was concerned with establishing law and order (šaltāniš ittallak). The unusual statement that 'the king (šarru) returned to his land'

---

[222] Wiseman 1956, 34; Thiele 1956, 26; Malamat 1956, 254.

[223] Ezek. 17:12 implies that Jehoiachin and the princes were taken there by Nebuchadrezzar himself.

[224] Malamat 1968, 146–50, n. 19–26; Thiele 1956, 22–7; Horn 1967, 12–27.

[225] To Malamat's list of those who do not follow the Tishri Calendar the detailed arguments in Clines 1972, 9–34 must be added.

[226] 2 Chron. 36:13–14 ('elohīm) cf. Ezek. 17:13–14, 19; Tsevat 1959, 199–204.

[227] Wiseman 1958, 31–59; Weinfeld 1976, 379–414.

[228] Wiseman 1956, 35–6, 72 (BM. 21946, r. 14′–15′); Grayson 1975, 102.

[229] Reading ul[tu xxx] since negative actions (Grayson 1975, 102 ul x) are rare except for āla ūl isbat (Grayson 1975, 82 l. 40; 89, l. 23; 92, ll. 17, 21).

may imply that the army was left in Syria to complete an as yet inconclusive seige.[230]

If the operations 'as far as Carchemish' should imply some disturbance in the north, the expedition in the following year up the bank of the Tigris may have been directed well east of Carehemish to Urartu, Elam/Zamua? as in Nabopolassar's eighteenth year. In 596/5 B.C. Nebuchadrezzar with his army encamped by the river a day's march from the enemy who panicked and turned back.[231] The name of the opponent is broken and my original suggestion that it was the 'king of Elam' (n[im.m]a.ki) is possible though doubtful.[231] In the time of Nabonidus Cyrus was called by the title 'king of Elam' in a dynastic prophecy text,[232] alongside the more conventional 'king of the Medes' and 'king of Parsu'.[233] However, Nebuchadrezzar claimed to rule over Marhaši[234] which lay to the north-west of Elam[235] and this campaign may be the first indication of the pressure from the eastern hill-people which was to be one major cause of the downfall of Babylon. In a prophecy dated early in the reign of Zedekiah Jeremiah said about Elam that following disaster her fortunes would be restored (Jer. 49: 34, 39).

Though Nebuchadrezzar was 'in his own land' for much of his tenth year the reason for this could have been the peaceful status of the conquered lands rather than internal strife. The rebellion (*bartu*) both by its description and duration, Kislev to Tebet (Dec/Jan 595/4 B.C.), was political rather than military, the text reading lú.gal.meš-*šu madūtu*, 'his numerous leading persons'/officials,[236] rather than 'he put his large (army) to the sword'.[237] The Chronicle implies that the enemy was an individual (*ayābišu*) who was captured by the king in person. The suggestion that the timing of the rebellion in Kislev was when the king was normally away on expedition to Hattu[238] is unlikely.

---

[230] *šarru* as subject occurs in BM. 21946, 10, otherwise the subject is expressed only in the verbal form, (BM. 21946, 20; 22047, 15) or in full as lugal *akkadi*[ki] (l. 21).

[231] Wiseman 1956, 72 (BM. 22047, r. 16–20 with possible restoration *ah i-diq-lat uš-ma* (cf. 1.2). Cf. Grayson 1975, 102.

[232] Grayson 1975A 32, ii 17, 20 (possibly an archaism).

[233] YOS 7 8:14.; cf. Gadd 1958, 58 i 42 (*šar ᵈmadaya*).

[234] Lambert 1965, 2 ll. 22–3 (broken).

[235] Cf. Edzard 1974, 128.

[236] Cf. Grayson 1975, 86 29.

[237] Grayson 1975, 102 22.

[238] Von Voigtlander 1964, 94.

Such an absence is unattested for the preceeding three years and it would have been a chancy assumption for any rebel to make. Moreover, it would have been unlikely, had this been the case, for the king to go abroad as he did in the following Kislev. There is no evidence that the revolt stemmed from the unceasing military expeditions of the previous fourteen years for these were sustained mainly by a mercenary force.

The Chronicle implies that the enemy was a person acting alone and the rebellion was quickly suppressed. The confiscation and disposal of the property of Babu-aha-iddina, son of Nabû-ahhē-bulliṭ, who was summarily tried, found guilty of breaking the loyalty-oath (implying that he was a high official) and condemned to death, confirms this.[239] Babu-aha-iddina's father had been granted lands near Borsippa as a special favour from Nabopolassar so was presumably an influential citizen. It has also been suggested that the rebellion involved some of the Judean deportees in Babylonia since Nebuchadrezzar also put to death by burning Ahab ben Kolaiyah and a Zedekiah ben-Maaseyah who had prophesied that the Jewish exile would last only two years in contrast to the seventy predicted by Jeremiah (29:21–22).

The Chronicle makes it clear that after the rebellion Nebuchadrezzar went once more to Hattu to receive the valuable tribute which 'the kings and the [subordinate governors of Ha]ttu[240] brought before him'. The wording is that of a formal reception of tribute which was taken back to Babylon. With the statement that in his eleventh year Nebuchadrezzar with his army was once more in Syria (Hattu) the extant Babylonian Chronicle texts for the reign come to an end.[241] The Egyptian attitude to Asia after 596 seems to be one of trying to consolidate its own position and of continuing its alliances with Phoenicia. Katzenstein may well be right to see in the recurrence of the phrase in 594/3 that Nebuchadrezzar 'mustered his troops' as a major call-up to demonstrate in force in Hattu against Egyptian

---

[239] Weidner 1954, 1–5; for the confiscation of a traitor's property after death see Alalakh Tablet No. 17 (ANET 546) and 1 Kings 21:13.

[240] BM. 21946, r. 23 (Wiseman 1956, 72) could be restored lugal me *u* lú.[en.nam].*tú*

[241] BM. 21901 r. 76–7 and BM. 22047, show that in *nishu*-texts the catchline normally consists of wording followed precisely in the initial line of the following tablet of the Chronicle.

plans for further opposition following the recent elevation of Psammetichus II to the throne.[242]

We are left to cull the picture of Nebuchadrezzar's remaining years from incidental references in Neo-Babylonian texts and extra-Babylonian sources. Since an astronomical diary for Nebuchadrezzar's thirty-eighth year has survived[243] there is no reason to doubt that this class of text, which traditionally goes back to the time of Nabû-nāṣir (Nabonasar), was kept regularly. The diaries often included historical notes taken from records which were one source of the information collected or abstracted, in the Babylonian Chronicles.[244]

From the Old Testament it seems that Zedekiah early in his reign challenged the Babylonian domination of the West.[245] He brought diplomatic representatives from as far afield as Tyre and Sidon, Edom, Moab and Ammon, but significantly not from the Philistinian cities, to Jerusalem (Jer. 27:1–11). Whether they had come to win him over to an anti-Babylonian coalition is not clear, though the original pressure could have come from the Egyptians through Psammetichus II who in 591 sailed to Byblos ostensibly on a religious pilgrimage.[246] Zedekiah seems to have acted independently, mindless of the fate of Jehoiakim and against the advice of Jeremiah, in withdrawing allegiance from Babylon.[247]

Nebuchadrezzar and the Final Seige of Jerusalem

Nebuchadrezzar's response was characteristically swift and bold. He used a large force to begin the attack on Jerusalem on the 10th of Tebet of Zedekiah's ninth year (15 Jan. 588 B.C., Jer 39:1; 2 Kings 25:1). Seige walls and works were built around it to prevent any movement in or out, much as had Sennacherib in the seige of the same city in 701.[248] This indicated the expectation of a long drawn out operation to starve the city into surrender. Zedekiah appealed to the new Egyptian king Apries

---

[242] Katzenstein 1973, 314.
[243] Weidner 1953, Tf. XVII (after p. 424; VAT 4956).; Sachs 1955, xii.
[244] Sachs 1948, 285–6; Wiseman 1956, 4; Grayson 1975, 13–14.
[245] *JBL* 76 (1957), 305; Freedy & Redford 1970, 475.
[246] Kienitz 1967, 269.
[247] Josephus *Antiq. Jud.* X vii 3–4.
[248] Siege towers were available (cf. BM. 21946, 22; Josephus, *Antiq. Jud.* X viii, 1).

(Ezek. 17:15) whose tentative response may have been with very moderate forces.[249] The approach to him may have been made by a military mission under Koriah, son of Elnathan, possibly the commander-in-chief of Judah according to the Lachish letters.[250] Any Egyptian advance caused but a temporary diversion of a few of the beseigers about a year after the commencement of the seige,[251] and it enabled a few to leave the city.[252] Nebuchadrezzar meanwhile worked steadily to eliminate support for Lachish and to cut off the hill-forts, especially to the south-west, by which route help might be expected.[253] Nevertheless a number of Judean forts established to keep watch on, or receive smoke or fire signals from, Lachish and Azekah appear to have been spared. Khirbet Abu et-Twein to the north of Jerusalem was one of these.[254] The seige was then tightened by the addition of a closer siege-wall and the bringing up of siege towers to make a breach in the (northern?) wall.[255] The break through happened on the 9th of Tammuz of Zedekiah's eleventh year, the Temple being destroyed in the following week, that is 7th or 10th Ab (c. 5 August 587) according to the Nisan year reckoning[256] and the city fell about a month later. The interval may well have been due to Babylonian attempts to parley for surrender (Jer 39:3). The western wall, part of the earlier well-fortified Israelite construction, was too formidable to be breached.[257]

There is some evidence that the population was in such dire straits as to have been forced to surrender through hunger.[258] Archaeological support for the destruction of Jerusalem at this time is difficult to trace because of subsequent rebuilding. Kenyon considered the city to have been destroyed and made uninhabitable and the destruction of houses on the eastern wall may be attributed to this seige.[259] Elsewhere in Judah towns like

---

[249] Jer. 37:5; Ezek. 17:17; Josephus *Antiq. Jud.* X 108–11; *JBL* 76 (1957), 308ff.

[250] Malamat 1968, 151–2; Freedy and Redford 1970, 480.

[251] Jer. 37: 5–11; cf. Lam. 4:17; Malamat 1968, 152 dates this to the end of winter/spring 587 B.C. on the basis of Ezek. 29:1; 30:20; 31:1.

[252] Jer. 34: 6–8; 38:19. This was the basis of the charge of desertion which led to Jeremiah's imprisonment (Jer. 24:1–2; 37:12, 21; 38:28; 39:12.)

[253] Jer. 34:7; Lachish Letter IV, 10–13.

[254] Mazar 1981, 229 ff.

[255] 2 Kings 25:1; Jer. 32:24; 33:4; cf. Ezek. 4:1–2; 22:22. Zedekiah's escape through the southern wall may have taken place at this time.

[256] Malamat 1968, 150 argues from the Tisri New Year dating for 15 August 586 B.C.

[257] *IEJ* 29 (1979), 90–1.

[258] Jer. 37:21; Cf. 2 Kings 6:24–7:4; Oppenheim 1955, 71–2.

[259] Kenyon 1976, 596; 1967, 104.

Lachish and Beth-Shemesh ceased to be inhabited at this time, and at Gezer and Tell el Hesi (VII/VI) an ash layer has been taken to be the result of Babylonian destruction there. But at Tell Beit Mirsim, Beth-Shemesh and Ramat Rahel some royal estates were left to supply wine to Babylon as they had previously to the royal household in Jerusalem.[260] These were administered by 'Eliakim, assistant of Jehoiachin' (*l'lyqm n'r ywkn*) from the name on jar-handles.[261] It is noteworthy that a number of stamp seal impressions found at sites in the Judean hills attest the dispersion of the Judean bureaucrats at this time. These include the seal of Ja'azaniah a royal official (*y'znyh 'bd hmlk*) found at Tell en-Nasbeh (Mizpah) which Gedaliah made his headquarters on his appointment as governor by the Babylonians and to which the pro-Babylonian Jeremiah was brought to help the effort to restore order (40:6). Gedaliah, who is generally identified with the prime-minister whose seal-impression (*lgdlyh 'šr 'l hbyt*) was found at Lachish. His appointment was typical of the Babylonian system of creating local native governorships. Also from outside Jerusalem have been recovered inscribed bullae of the scribe Baruch (*lbrkyhw bn nryhw hspr*, 'belonging to Berechiah, son of Neriah, the scribe' and of 'Jerahmeel the king's son' (*lyrhm'l bn hmlk*) together with the seals of office of others mentioned in Jeremiah 36. Jerahmeel was also a royal official and may be identified with the person who burned Jeremiah's scroll (Jer. 36:26) Baruch may also have been a state employee in addition to his work as private secretary to Jeremiah.[262]

Efforts to restore the shattered province of Judah were thwarted by the murder of Gedaliah by supporters of the old royal house. Their fear of Babylonian reprisals indicates that it would be the normally expected consequences of such action which the conspirators sought to evade by escaping to Egypt taking Jeremiah with them (Jer 42:1–22). Yet Babylonian reprisals came in 582/1 B.C. when Nebuzaradan the commander of the Imperial Guard took a further 745 Judeans into exile and

---

[260] *JBL* 51 (1932), 77–106; *AASOR* 12 (1932) 78; cf. *EI* 15 (1981), 140–4 for similar royal estates supplying wine earlier from Jezreel. See now J.N. Graham, *BA* 47 (1944) 55–8 Mizpah, Gibeon and Mozah, north of Jerusalem.

[261] C.C. McCown, *Tell en-Nasbeh I* (1947), pl. 57. 4; S. Moscati, *L'epigrafia ebraica antica 1935–1950* (1951) 70.

[262] Avigad 1979, 115–7.

Judah is presumed to have been annexed to the province of Samaria (Jer 52:30). This further action is also known from Josephus who records that in this year Nebuchadrezzar 'made an expedition against Coele-Syria and, when he had possessed himself of it, he made war against the Ammonites and Moabites; and when he had brought all these nations under subjection, he fell upon Egypt, in order to overthrow it; and he slew the king that then reigned and set up another; and he took those Jews that were there captives and led them away to Babylon.'[263] As it is thought that this could not have been carried out in a single year[264] this may have been a general summary of Nebuchadrezzar's operations. Hophra was supplanted by Ahmose II (Amasis) in 570, if it is these kings and not those of Judah to whom Josephus actually refers. The later Arabic tradition (Tabari) was that the Babylonian invasion of Egypt resulted from Nebuchadrezzar's desire to capture fugitive Jews and to achieve his aim peacefully.[265]

Against Egypt

Other than the reference to a Babylonian attack on Egypt in the post-587 B.C. prophecies of Jeremiah (43:8–13) given in Tahpanhes (Tell Defneh), there is little evidence for it. Jeremiah told of the king of Babylon coming to set up his throne and pavilion at the entrance to the royal palace there. He assumes that the conquest would result in destruction of Egyptian temples including that of Beth-Shemesh (Heliopolis).[266] Moreover, the suggestion that the brick pavement excavated at Tell Defneh was the putative throne-base[267] is not confirmed and no inscriptions of Nebuchadrezzar originating in Egypt have yet been found there.[268]

However, a fragmentary cuneiform text (BM. 33041) which includes a reference to 'Nebuchadrezzar's thirty-seventh year'

[263] Josephus, *Antiq. Jud.* X ix, 7.

[264] Von Voigtlander 1964, 113–14; the war against the trans-Jordanian tribes (Josephus, *Antiq. Jud.* X. 181–2) perhaps repeated the early foray there in 599 B.C. (Spalinger 1977, 236).

[265] Tabari X 181–2; references in Spalinger 1977, 237 n. 58.

[266] LXX 'which are in On'.

[267] W.M. Flinders Petrie, 'Defennes (Tahpanhes)' in *Tanis* II (1888) 50–1; S.R. Driver, *The Book of Jeremiah* (1908), 258 n.*f.*

[268] The cylinders of Nebuchadrezzar II in the Cairo Museum are building inscriptions from Babylon and therefore probably imports (information from Dr. K.A. Kitchen).

could refer to an invasion of Egypt against Amasis two years
earlier in 570 B.C. when Amasis was at war with Cyrene with
whom he was later allied.[269] The Babylonian text[270] appears to
have had a hymnal preface so the precise genre is uncertain. The
text seems to refer to Amasis (*[Am]asu*) as king of Egypt (*šar
mi-ṣir*), and to Necho (*[Ni?]-ku-ú*) who had (captured?) the
town of Putu-Yaman, to 'remote territories in the middle of the
sea' (r.l. 3) and 'weapons, horses, chariots he summoned to his
help.' The objective of the expedition is specified as 'to do battle
with Egypt' (*[ana* ^*māt*^*] miṣir ana epēš tahazi il[lik]*). Spalinger
argues that, since the location of and indeed the reference to,
Putu-Yaman is unsure, it is not possible to read here any
reference to an invasion of Egypt.[271] Though later traditions
made Nebuchadrezzar the conqueror of Libya and even as far as
Iberia[272] it is likely that some of these sources reflect confusion
with Cambyses' later invasion. The Coptic story of Cambyses,
like the Ethiopian version of the Chronicle of John, Bishop of
Nikiu, follows an anti-Apries tradition. However, the dating of
this folk-romance back to the reign of Nebuchadrezzar seems
secure.[273] The British Museum text may relate to an incident in
the last years of the reign of Apries and beginning of that of
Amasis when there was civil war in Egypt in 570 B.C. following
the failure of Apries to capture the Greek colony of Cyrene.
This troubled period is also reflected in other later classical
traditions.[274] It is likely that any invasion of Egypt by
Nebuchadrezzar must have taken place before this, probably in
the reign of Apries. It has also been suggested that the tribute
given by Egypt to an unnamed Babylonian king could date from
this reign,[275] but against this is the Babylonian's claim to have
been sovereign over the Medes.[276] The same text also implies that
the kings of Hattu and Egypt had 'to give definite orders to bring
in 1,000 talents of silver, 1,000 talents of gold, 1,000 talents of

---

[269] Herodotus II 161–2, 181: Drioton 1952, 567–8.

[270] Wiseman 1956, 94–5, pl. xx–xxi; Malamat 1973, 278; Langdon 1912, 206–7.

[271] Spalinger 1977, 238. Malamat (*JANES* 5 (1973) 278) argues that the text has nothing to do
with a campaign in 568 BC but is rather a broken list of foreign mercenary contingents in
Babylonian service (cf. Berger 1973, 6).

[272] Megasthenes in Josephus, *Contra Apionem* I, 20.

[273] Spalinger 1977, 240.

[274] Herodotus II 161f.; IV, 159; Diodorus I, 68.

[275] Spalinger 1977, 240.

[276] Wiseman 1967, 496; cf. Spalinger *ibid*.

choice selected antimony; 10,000 talents in ingots of copper, 1,000 talents in bricks of lead, 6,000 half bricks or drums of tin; 10,000 bales of dark blue wool; 10,000 bales of (violet) purple wool; 10,000 bales of bright red wool; 5,000 garments for officials . . .' Such major supplies to Babylon betoken an initial tribute following a special sweep by 'the guard-troops watching over Kaldu and Aramu' and may not be applicable to this period so much as to the succeeding Achaemenians.

Although extant sources do not afford sufficient evidence for tracing the exact chronological development there can be no question that during his reign Nebuchadrezzar justified his use of the general and traditional claim of his building inscriptions that his sway held 'from the upper to the lower seas'.[277] It stretched from Egypt in the south-west through Syro-Palestine to Cilicia, Pirindu and Lydia in the north-west. His claim to have conquered such distant regions (*šar nagî nesûtim*)[278] would cover his operations into the Taurus foot-hills and as far as Elam which, though now lost in the text BM. 45690, are areas named in other cuneiform sources.[278] It is not unlikely that Nebuchadrezzar considered himself 'king of kings' (*šar šarrāni* cf. Daniel 2:37), a title used by his successors.[279]

What is remarkable is that in the space of thirty-five years at the most Nebuchadrezzar had gained an 'empire' larger than that lost by Ashurbanipal of Assyria only ten years earlier. Not only so but his skilfully planned operations were followed up by a series of measures to govern and ensure law and order of the traditional Babylonian type. Harshness was mingled with mercy which made the Babylonian overlordship acceptable to many though deadly for the independence of most.

[277] Langdon 1912, 46 iii 2, 5.
[278] Lambert 1965, 2, 6 (BM. 45690 r. v. 20–4).
[279] *šar šarrāni* occurs as early as Middle Babylonian as an alternative to the title *šarru rabû* (e.g. KUB 37 139:5).

II

BABYLON

It must not be thought that Nebuchadrezzar's only major effort was the military and judicial activity essential to the speedy recovery and control of the widespread 'empire' taken over by Babylon as heir to the formidable Assyrians. His inscriptions, perhaps because the majority which survive are of the category of so-called 'building inscriptions', lay the emphasis on the rebuilding work he undertook at Babylon and in twelve cities at various locations in Babylonia. One stated and major purpose of his campaigns in the west was to bring back booty and expert prisoner-of-war labour for the enrichment of his capital city. Here the evidence for the nature and extent of his activities in Babylon is re-examined.

'Is not this the great Babylon which I have built as the royal residence by my mighty power and for the glory of my majesty?' (Dan 4:30) is the declaration made by Nebuchadrezzar as he was walking on the roof of the royal palace at Babylon (Dan 4:30). While 'great' (Aram. *rabbᵉtâ*) is here but a general term, it is to be noted that in the Old Testament the adjective 'great' (*gdl*) before 'city' is used to point to the status of an 'important' royal capital (Gibeon, Josh 10:2; Jerusalem, Jer 22:8; Nineveh, Jonah 1:2; 3:2; cf. 4:11) and not necessarily to emphasise its colossal size.[1] The Aramaic *bᵉnâ*, as its counterpart Hebrew *banâ*, is used of both building and rebuilding.

For the confederation of Chaldaean tribes, as for the earlier Hebrews under David, the provision of a centre for government and administration and thus of a mercantile as well as a dominant cult centre was pressing. Previous attempts to centralise rule over the southern tribes at Babylon under Marduk-apla-iddina of the Bit-Yakin tribe had been thwarted by local dissention and opposition from some townsfolk and he had had to make his base outside at Borsippa nearer his supporting tribes.[2] When Nabopolassar ousted the Assyrian-dominated

---

[1] Wiseman 1979, 35–6.
[2] Cf. Brinkman 1964, 14, 18.

rulers of Babylonia he chose Babylon as his seat and governed
from a small palace on the citadel close by the Ishtar gate. The
choice was probably made on the basis of the long tradition of
Babylon as 'the centre of the world'. His first task in 627 BC was
the restoration of the walls. There is no record of any work done
in the city by its last Assyrian governor Kandalanu, and back to
the fall of the city after a long seige and famine there in 648 B.C.
Ashurbanipal and Šamaš-šum-ukīn had made only minor repairs
to the walls and the two main temples.[3]

Babylon's Origin

The origin of Babylon is obscure, but according to the
Babylonian Chronicle and omens relating back to Sargon of
Agade (*c.* 2350 B.C.) that king claims to have removed rubble or
dust from a clay pit at Babylon and heaped it up near, or in front
of, Agade naming it Babylon.[4] Such a gesture is elsewhere
attested as marking the conquest of an existing city[5] rather than,
as is usually interpreted, denoting the establishment of a new
one.[6] Since Sargon by this claims to have set up 'the likeness of
Babylon' (gaba.ri *bābili*)[7] the name, and thus the reality, was
held to have been in use earlier.[8] His action was considered evil,
possibly as defiling a revered sacred site,[9] and for it his dynasty
was thought to have been brought to an end.[10] The reference
there to the source of building materials, as in Gilgamesh's
Uruk, may further indicate that the original city was both
extensive and a religious centre.[11]

Though Babylon seems to have had only a limited rôle under
a local governor in the Ur III period[12] it flourished as the capital

---

[3] Streck 1916, 236–8 (L[6]:13–24); 230 L[2] 12 (Esagil and Etemenanki); 242 S[2] 33–6 (Ezida).

[4] Grayson 1975, 152–3 (Babylonian Chronicle 20 A 17–19).

[5] D.D. Luckenbill, *The Annals of Sennacherib* (1924) 136 46 (Babylon); cf. Borger 1956, 116 ii 11–13 (Arina); Streck 1916, 56 vi 96–8 (Susa); King 1907 II 8; J. Nougayrol, 'Note sur la place des "présages historiques" dans l'extispicine babylonienne', in *École Practique des Hautes Études: Annuaire* (1944–5) 1–3.

[6] Grayson 1975, 47, 153.

[7] King 1907 II 8:18.

[8] A tradition reflected in Gen. 11:1–9.

[9] For the rites defining the foundation of a sacred site see Ellis 1968, 12–15.

[10] As was that of Sennacherib following his destruction of Babylon in 689 B.C. (Brinkman 1973, 94).

[11] Cf. The Epic of Gilgamesh XI 307 (*issû*).

[12] Sollberger 1979.

of a powerful Amorite clan among whom Hammurapi had an international reputation.[13] This dominant position, despite a raid by the Hittites *c.* 1595 B.C. and destruction by Sennacherib in 689 B.C. was never lost. All who controlled it accorded it respect as the ancient foundation – 'the eternal city' (*āl šubat dārâti*) – which had early become the traditional capital.[14]

The Name

When Šar-kali-šarri, son of Naram-Sīn rebuilt the temple of Anunītum and Ilaba there he referred to Babylon by its Sumerian designation ká.dingir.ki or the fuller and more frequent name of ká.dengir.ra.ki i.e. 'Gate of God'.[15] Whether this denoted the place of entry into the deity's presence or even the gate as the place of divine judgement or both is uncertain. Should this be the original name, Babylon is unique in that no other place in ancient Mesopotamia is designated either by its function or by an Akkadian translation of a Sumerian geographical name, *bāb-ili*.[16] Even if the latter is taken to be merely *Volksetymologie*[17] this would then be shown to go back at least to Akkadian times.[18] The occurrence of other logographic writings of the city name (ká.diš.diš) = *Bāb-ilān*)) in the reign of Esarhaddon[19] and Ashurbanipal[20] may merely be instances of scribal idiosyncrasies. Though the syllabic spelling *ba-bi-lu/i* is rare,[21] it is likely that the reading *bāb-ilāni* 'Gate of the gods' or *bāb-ilān* (dual), 'gate of the two gods'[22] from which the Greeks took the name βαβυλών as early as the seventh century B.C. is of earlier origin. The suggestion that the name *Bāb-ili* may also be a play on *bāb-elli* 'Holy gate' is unlikely.[23]

---

[13] Renger 1979, 208; CAH II/I (1973) 176–90.

[14] *RA* 29 (1932) 98 l. 4; see also Langdon 1912, 172 viii 23; 258 ii.11.

[15] Thureau-Dangin 1907, 225; for the construct form Dūr-ili see *RA* 13 (1916) 21; and for Bāb- compounded with a geographical name Parpola 1970A 57–64.

[16] Gelb 1955, 1–2.

[17] As is commonly argued for Gen. 11:7–9 and the derivation *bālal*//*bābel*.

[18] Trenkvalder 1979, 237; however her reading of tab.tab.dingir.ki as 'Viergotterstadt' on the analogy of tab.tab.dingir: *arba'ili* (also written tab.tab.diš.ki) is unlikely as the reading Bāb-ilim occurs from Ur III onwards.

[19] Borger 1956, 30–1.

[20] Streck 1916, 244, 22.

[21] ABL 878, 8, 10; 848 r.47.

[22] Borger 1956, 31.

[23] *RlA* I 361c.

Since the logogram d/tin.tir.ki is frequently used in correspondence and judicial and official texts from the time of Shalmaneser III[24] it is possible that this was also a common name used for the city as *pars pro toto*[25] The meaning of d/tin.tir.ki is still uncertain there being no occurrence with giš.tir (*qištu*=wood) to support the correspondence made with tir Babilla forest in the Lagash region mentioned in Ur III texts.[26] However, a text dated in Uruk in Nebuchadrezzar's twenty-third year mentions both tin.tir.ki and nun.ki, the latter also a rare designation of a city quarter.[27] The same applied to Šu.an.na used as a reference to Babylon by Sargon and Ashurbanipal.[28]

Neo-Babylonian contracts predominantly use e.ki, possibly meaning 'canal-area' – itself perhaps an abreviation of the city quarter te.e.ki. The unusual name *šešak* in Jeremiah 25:26; 31:41, though commonly explained as an Atbash cypher for *bbl*, could be an erudite rendering of the title šeš.kù[29] or ùru. (=šeš). kù, 'holy city.'[30]

These names are included in the Topography of Babylon, a scholastic composition entitled tin. tir. ki = *ba-bi-lu*;[31] a series of texts more complete than the other extant topographies of cult centres at Assur[32] and Uruk.[33] It is thought to have been composed as early as the time of Nebuchadrezzar I[34] in whose reign the city and its god took a pre-eminent place following the recovery of the stolen statue of Marduk from Elam.[35] The text was copied in scribal schools at Kish, Sippar, Uruk and Ur and, as would be expected, mainly in Babylon itself, at least until the first century B.C. when an exemplar survives in Greek.[36] The series of five tablets has now been largely reconstructed by

---

[24] Parpola 1970A, 58–64.
[25] For its use in this manner see p. 49.
[26] Renger 1979, 208.
[27] Lutz 1927, I 42.
[28] VAB 7 262 32; 148 22; R.C. Thompson, *The Prisms of Esarhaddon and of Ashurbanipal* (1931) 30, 26; A.G. Lie, *The Inscriptions of Sargon II, king of Assyria* I (1929) 58 15.
[29] *RA* 24 (1927) 184f.
[30] T.G. Pinches, *PSBA* 2 (1880) 22; 22 (1900) 370.
[31] E. Unger in Wetzel 1930, pl. 82; Unger 1931, 229 ff.; *AfO* 13 (1931) 124–7: *Iraq* 5 (1938), 55–64; CT 51 (1972) 92; *ZA* 41 (1972) 287ff.; Gurney 1974; George 1979, 226.
[32] KAVI Nr. 42–4.
[33] A. Falkenstein, *Topographie von Uruk* I (Leipzig 1941).
[34] George 1979, 232.
[35] Lambert 1964, 10.
[36] T.G. Pinches & A.H. Sayce *PSBA* 24 (1902) 108–24; *Iraq* 24 (1962) 67–8.

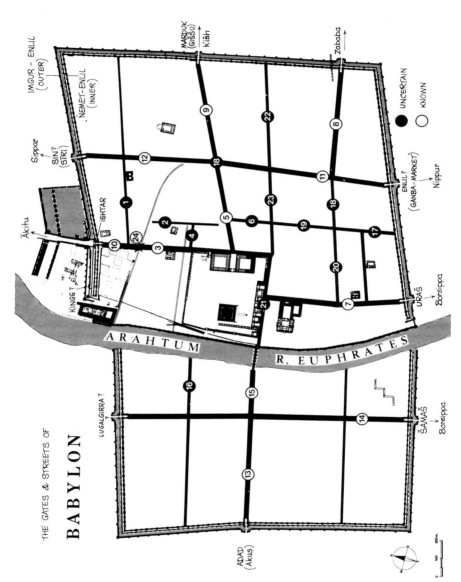

THE GATES & STREETS OF

BABYLON

FIG. 3. Walls, gates and streets of Babylon

KEY TO FIG. 3

Babylonian name (*sūqu*)	Street name
1. *išēmê šē'ašu*	He will hear the one who seeks him
2. *kunuš kadru qatnu*	Bow down, proud one! (Narrow Street)
3. *āy-ibur-šabû sūqu rapšu*	May the arrogant not flourish. (Broad Street)
4. *ṭâbi[. . .]laluma*	Good. . . .
5. *ayu ilu kī ᵈMarduk*	What god is like Marduk?
6. *tana[r] giššu*	Giššu
7. *Nabû dayān nīšišu sūq abul ᵈUraš*	Nabû, judge of his people, street of the Uraš gate
8. *ᵈzababa muhalliq sūq abul ᵈZababa*	Zababa, destroyer of his enemies, street of the Zababa gate.
9. *ᵈMarduk rē'i mātišu sūq abul giššu*	Marduk, shepherd of his country, street of the Giššu gate
10. *ᵈIštar lamassi ummanišu sūq abul ᵈištar*	Ishtar, intercessor for her men (people), street of the Ishtar gate
11. *ᵈenlil mukîn šarrūtišu sūq abul ᵈenlil*	Enlil, establisher of his kingship, street of the Enlil gate
12. *ᵈSin mukîn agē bēlūtišu sūq abul ᵈSin*	Sin, establisher of his royal crown, street of the Sin gate
13. *ᵈadad zānin nīšišu sūq abul ᵈAdad*	Adad, provider for his people, street of the Adad gate
14. *ᵈšamaš ṣulul ummanišū sūq abul ᵈšamaš*	Shamash, protector of his men, street of the Shamash gate
15. *kurub lišmēka*	Pray and he will hear you
16. *mê usu*	Bring down(?) the waters
17. *sūq damiq-ilišu*	Street of Damiq-ilišu
18. *sūq erbetti*	Crossroads
19. *sūq ᵈsibitti*	Pleiades street
20. *sūq ili maštabba*	Gemini street
21. *sūq hudda mātsu*	Make glad his country street
22. *ṭassu karabi*	. . . greeting
23. *išemû ana rūqu*	He listens to the distant one
24. *sulā marduk*	Highway of Marduk

George.[37] This enables a comparison between the religious view of the city and its divine inhabitants which is elsewhere incorporated into the hymnic literature and the reality recorded both in Nebuchadrezzar's own building records and the site as partially unearthed in excavations by the German expedition 1899–1914, and the State Organisation for Antiquities and Heritage of Iraq in 1974–83.

[37] A. George, *The Series Tintir = Bābilu and the Topography of Babylon* (University of Birmingham Ph.D. 1984, unpublished).

Tablet I lists the literary names of Babylon in Sumerian with their Akkadian translation or etymological interpretation. Tablet II of the series gives the dwelling-place (*šubtu*) within the city of each deity, in a few instances with their location or with notes.

Tablet IV was probably occupied with a list of the 43 *māhāzu*, i.e. cult places or places of prayer,[38] and their occupants in Babylon (*māhāzi ilāni^mes^ rabûti^mes^ libbi bābili*). Indications are given of the city-quarter within which they were located. The text emphasises the symbolic or cosmological importance attached to the main shrines,[39] a fact to which each restorer of them, Esarhaddon,[40] Ashurbanipal,[41] Nabopolassar,[42] and Nebuchadrezzar, refers.

Tablet V, lists the throne-daises (*parakku*) of Marduk or possibly the named shrines within Marduk's temple complex of *Esa(n)gil(a)* (ll. 1–47). There follow the names of the eight city-gates (Uraš, Zababa, Marduk, Ištar, lugal (King), Adad and Šamaš (ll. 49–56); the inner *Imgur-^d^Enlil* ('Enlil was gracious') and outer (*šalhu*) wall, *nemet-^d^enlil* ('Rampart of Enlil' ll. 57–8); the R. Euphrates (Arahtum – 'river of Abundance' l. 59) and the main canals (*nārē*) named Huduk [. . .], the Libil-hegalla and a feeder canal (*atap Šamaš*).

The Topography continues with the names of twenty-four streets of Babylon,[43] eight of which are related to the eight gates named earlier in this text and can therefore be located with reasonable certainty. Apart from the broad Procession Street (*Ai-ibur-šabû*) the rest are not mentioned in texts in sufficient detail to be placed on any city map other than on the assumption that the streets were laid out on a grid pattern, hitherto unattested for an ancient Babylonian city (Fig. 3).[44]

The topography summarises the distinctive topographical features (*bunnannû*) of Babylon (ll. 83–9) as '43 cult-centres

---

[38] *Or* 43 (1974) 83, 86

[39] Gurney 1974, 46 l. 83.

[40] Borger 1956, 21 ll. 47–51.

[41] Streck 1916, 228 ll. 13–16; 236 ll. 5–19; 242 ll. 26–45.

[42] Langdon 1912, 64 Nr 1 iii 41–61; 68 Nr 4. 34–40.

[43] The number 24 can be justified by assuming that names are lost at the ends of ll. 62, 75 and that *sula ^d^Marduk* is the name of a distinctive highway, perhaps part of the Procession Street. SBH 142 iii.11 refers only to 2 roads (*girrī*) and 8 gates, For the Inner Wall see Kamel 1979.

[44] For the walls reconstructed by Nebuchadrezzar see Langdon 1912, 1 ii 12–21, 33–5; 84 Nr. 5 i 12–18.

(*māhāzi*) of the great gods of Babylon; 300 chapels or 'holy-places' (*parakku*) of the Igigi and 600 chapels of the A (nunnaki);

180 open-air shrines (*ibrat*) of Ishtar.
180 'stations' (*manzaz*) of Lugalirra and Meslamtea;
12 'stations' of the Pleiades (Sibitti);
6 'stations' of Pisces (*zibbāti*);
2 'stations' of [. . .]
2 'stations' of ᵈra[. . .] and Babylon [. . .]'

It concludes with a description of the six districts on the east bank;

'Eridu (as the district) in which Esagil (is built);
From the Market Gate (*abul mahīri*) to the Sublime Gate (*abulli ṣīri*) is (the area of) Tê;
From the Market Gate to the Uraš Gate is Dintir
From the Sublime Gate to the Ištar Gate is Bābili
From the Ištar Gate to the temple of Bēlet-Eanna [on the bank of the canal . . . is . . .]
From the gate of the temple of Bēlet-Eanna on the bank [of the canal to . . . is . . .]' (ll. 91–7)
The four districts of the West Bank:-
(From the) temple of Adad to the Akuṣ Gate, its name is Nuhar-parki;
From Akuṣ gate to the mortuary temple (é. nam. úš), [the *area*] in which the Ešmah temple is built, its name is Kumar;
From the middle of the arch (*abunnat* ⁱˢ *qašti*) of the gate of the temple of Bēlet-Ninâ to the bank of the river, its name is Lugal-Girra Gate;
From the Šamaš Gate to the river, its name is Tuba[45]; (ll. 98–102)
The total: Ten districts (*ālāni* ᵐᵉˢ) whose surrounding fields are fertile.
References to some of these districts occur in texts.[46] For some local administrative purposes subdivisions or another

[45] Variant Tubi. For an ancient plan of a wall and water at Tubaᵏⁱ see CT22 49, (BM. 3538).
[46] E.g. Nemet-Nejat 1982, 92 No. 24 r. 5 uru.gibil.ki *šá* ki[kù].ga (dated 499 B.C.); 52 No. 8 r. 1 (uru e [. . .]); 25 r. 1 (*ālu šá bit naš paṭri/ṭabihi*)
[47] George 1979, 230.

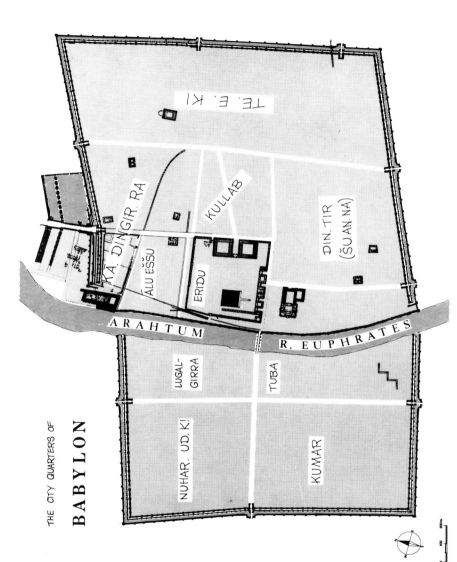

THE CITY QUARTERS OF
BABYLON

Fig. 4. City-quarters or administrative districts of Babylon

nomenclature was employed.[47] The location of the main quarters or administrative districts of Babylon is given in Fig. 4.

Nebuchadrezzar's Building Activities in Babylon

Unlike the dated Assyrian royal building inscriptions the cylindrical form of commemorative deposit favoured by the Neo-Babylonians does not provide chronological evidence for the various operations mentioned.[48] Since his military expeditions to Syria and the west resulted in the acquisition of much spoil including massive cedars specifically taken for reconstruction work it is likely that one of Nebuchadrezzar's early concerns was the repair of the main river wall and quay to receive this. The delapidation here had resulted in flood damage to the city walls, streets and the sacred temple precincts despite the earlier work of Nabopolassar. Nebuchadrezzar set in hand a series of hydraulic works which, with the extended quay-walls to counter the drift of the R. Euphrates eastwards and the net-work of canals across the city, formed a unique building feat comparable only with that undertaken by Sennacherib at Nineveh. The R. Euphrates was used to bring in goods along this low cost communication line from upstream and this made necessary the development of the quay on the city river bank through which goods, passengers or pilgrims could land.[49] The river and moat and walls, or escarpment, repaired by Nabopolassar on the east bank were flanked and covered by Nebuchadrezzar's work of reinforcement.[50] The quay at 1.4 m. above high water level served as a dock with stairways leading from the town level to it, with others descending further to at least –4.90 m. below to allow access to the river at low-water level. The refurbished Libil-hegalla canal 2.70 m. wide served both for water supply and as drainage from the Southern citadel which abutted its northern boundary. The entrance to the canal was provided with an iron grill as a defence against illegal entry, as were the outlets of other canals and drainage systems at the gateways.

Nebuchadrezzar's major building of the Western Outwork, which in effect diverted the river westwards and later

[48] Berger 1973, 108 (on the only three dated Neb. inscriptions).
[49] Bergamini 1981, 114.
[50] Wetzel 1930, pp. 30–6, pls. 42–4.

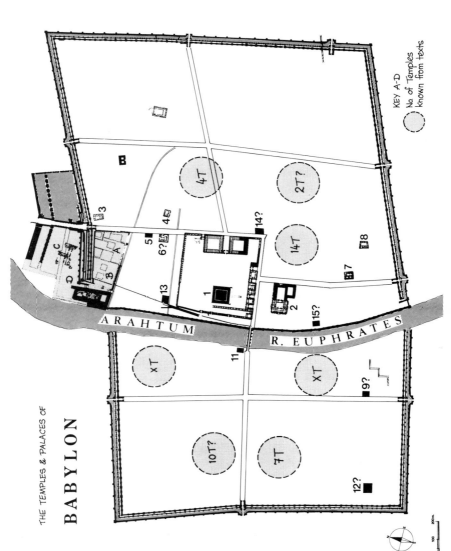

THE TEMPLES & PALACES OF
BABYLON

KEY A–D
No. of Temples
known from texts

Fig. 5. Temples and Palaces of Babylon

Palaces
A Nabopolassar
B Nebuchadrezzar II
C Nebuchadrezzar N. Palace
D. *halṣu rabîtu* – extension (*kummu*)
with gardens.

Temples
1. Etemenanki (ziggurat)
2. Esagila (Marduk)
3. é.mah (Ninmah-Bēlet ilī)
4. é.maš.dari (Ištar of Agade)

5. é. níg.gidri.kalam.ma.sum.ma
(Nabû ša harē)
6. é.kituš.kirzalla (Bēlet Eanna)
7. é.ša-.gar.tur.ra (Išhara)
8. é.PA.TU.til.la (Ninurta)
9. é.di.ku$_6$.kalam.ma (Šamaš)
10. .é.nam.hé (Adad?)
11. é.hursag.an.ki.a (Bēlet Ninâ)
12. é.nam.uš (Mortuary Temple)
13. é.hi.li.kalam.ma (Ašratum)
14. *bit rēš akīti*
15. é.kar.zagin.na

Other named temples are grouped within the city quarters under general total.

necessitated the rebuilding of the river wall in the east bank by Nabonidus, changed the shape of the city. It provided a protection for the raised platform on which Nebuchadrezzar built his great private residence (*kummu rabâ*).[51] The great citadel wall (*halṣi rabîti*)[52] was laid on a foundation of baked brick and bitumen set in the river.[53] The purpose was both to divert the river from eroding the bank by the royal palace and the Esagil shrine and to enable the whole of the base platform used for reconstruction on these sites to be set above the normal high river-level. To make this effective the northern city wall and gates had to be protected by a new outer and moat wall of burnt brick to replace the earlier escarpment of mud brick. The whole of the N. Citadel and W. Outwork had a new platform constructed of burnt brick and bitumen from below water level to just above it (Fig. 5).[54]

While this work was in hand Nebuchadrezzar resided in the east wing of the palace built by his father. This he had first to restore, since the foundation had subsided and the doors leading to the street had fallen. To the west of Nabopolassar's palace Nebuchadrezzar designed a palace for his own use since he 'did not have a royal residence (*nemēdi šarrūtiya*) in any other

---

[51] Langdon 1912, 21 ii 28–30.
[52] Probably the Western Outwork. There is no certainty that *halṣu* is a synonym for fort (*Or* 35 (1966) 313; *Bi.Or.* 32 (1975) 71).
[53] Berger 1973, 293; Koldewey 1914, 180.
[54] Langdon 1912, 117 Nr. 14 ii 2 (cf. CAD 2 (1965) 269).

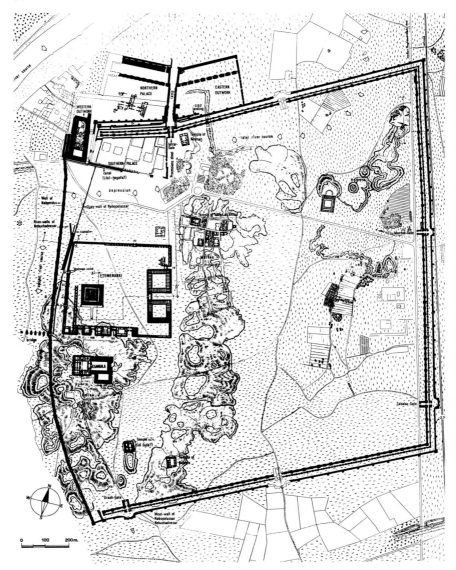

FIG. 6. Plan of excavations at Babylon (adapted from Bergamini 1977)

city'.[55] The kings of Babylonia before Nabopolassar 'used to build palaces and establish residences wherever they pleased, and stored their possessions in them and piled up their belongings there and only in the New Year Festival came to Babylon to please Marduk'.[56] Nebuchadrezzar's immediate aim was to unite Babylonia administratively. The finished palace he describes as 'a palace as the seat of my royal authority, a building for the admiration of my people, a place of union for the land' (*ekal bīti tabrâti nīši markasa māti*).[57] The area chosen was called *erṣet bābīli* (ká.dingir.ra) the original ('Southern') Citadel. The construction was magnificent, the upper walls were decorated all round with a band of blue enamelled bricks[58] and the doors made of cedar, Magan, sissoo[59] or ebony-wood encased in bronze or inlaid with silver, gold and ivory.[60] The doorway ceilings coated with lapis lazuli and the threshhold, lintel and architraves (*askuppī u nukusse*) cast in bronze.[61] The rooms themselves were roofed with huge cedar beams from Lebanon, or with selected pine and cypress logs, some covered in gold.[62] This palace, first systematically excavated by the German expedition under Koldewey, is currently being re-excavated and restored by the Iraqis.[63]

This palace naturally included the large private residence (*kummu rabû*) of the king which overlooked the quay wall and included sleeping accommodation.[64] Similar secluded rooms (*kummu*) were constructed in temples nearby[65] and atop the temple-tower.[66] Sennacherib at Nineveh built the *kummu* of his palace with columns of wood.[67] The *kummu* was also the site of

---

[55] ibid. 116 Nr. 14 ii 22.

[56] ibid. 114 Nr. 14 i 46.

[57] ibid. 136 Nr. 15 vii 36.

[58] ibid. 138 Nr. 15 ix.17; 118 Nr. 14. ii 46 (*kilīli uqnî rēšāša ušalmī*).

[59] *An.st.* 33 (1983) 67–62 Dalbergia Sissoo Roxburgh (cf. *BSOAS* 19 (1959) 317–8), found in Oman; the translation Magan-sissoo is used here, for if this were a wood imported from the East (as CAD 10 (1977) 237 sub *musukkannu*) it must be noted that Nebuchadrezzar also claims to have felled these himself, along with cedars, (VAS 1 45:4).

[60] ušû-wood = ebony (?); Langdon 1912, 119 Nr 14 ii 43; cf. ibid. 60 Nr. 1:43 for use of similar wood by Nabopolassar.

[61] Langdon 1912, 116 Nr.14 ii 17; 136 Nr. 15 viii 7; Berger 1975, 202:42.

[62] Langdon 1912, 119 Nr. 14 ii 44; Koldewey 1914, 169.

[63] Ali 1979, 92–3.

[64] Langdon 1912, 118 Nr. 21 ii 28–30; 116 Nr.14 ii.36; 138 Nr.15 viii 54; *HUCA* 38 (1967) 53.

[65] ibid. 226 Nr.1 iii. 16 (Nabonidus)

[66] ibid. 98 Nr.11 ii.4 contra Wetzel, 1938, 80.

[67] Luckenbill 1924, 110 vii 39; 123:36.

some intimate royal rituals. The association of these private quarters with the royal gardens may be indicated by the reference to the *halṣi rabîti* made by Nebuchadrezzar to be 'like a mountain.'[68] Similarly the palace gardens at Nineveh were compared with 'the likeness of the Amanus mountains' (*tamšil Hamani*) and were of a type depicted on the reliefs of the northern palace of Ashurbanipal (see Plate Ia).[69] This shows that such gardens were crowned with trees, and a small royal pavilion, kiosk or 'summer-house' (*bîtānu*).[70] That term may also denote the area within the palace walls, as opposed to the *kīdānu*, the open squares outside them. Similar pavilions were an integral part of the royal residences at Persepolis[71] and Susa[72] as of later oriental palaces.

The Palace Gardens

The location of royal gardens was usually close to the king's palace and, for privacy, had access through the double city-walls, to larger parklands. This was the case in contemporary Jerusalem where Zedekiah was able to make an escape through the walls (2 Kings 25:4–5; Jer. 39:4; 52:7). It is not impossible that the elaborate precautions taken against flooding and damp, using burnt bricks, asphalt and matting, between the Western Outwork and the palace proper along a narrow ditch flanked by drainage holes were part of a garden structure. This led down to a gateway at the junction with the main wall protected by a tower with a well in its inner revetment. Here was 'one large doorway in front and two small ones at the sides, an unusual arrangement not found elsewhere in Babylon. The whole was subsequently filled in as a base for the later Persian *apadana*, perhaps the work of Xerxes, built over it.'[73]

According to a cylinder inscription, between the Western Outwork and the northern palace Nebuchadrezzar 'formed

---

[68] Langdon 106 Nr. 13 ii 24, cf. 86 Nr. 7 ii.16.
[69] Barnett 1976, 14, pl. xxiii; though the reference here may be to an Elamite city not to the Amanus cf. pls. XVI–XIX.
[70] Wiseman 1983, 137–8; cf. Oppenheim 1965, 330–1.
[71] Schmidt 1953, pls 21, 24; fig. 3; E. Herzfeld, *Archäologische Mitteilungen Aus Iran* I.10.
[72] Esther 7:7–8 (*ginnat habbîtān*) cf. AhwB131b 'Innengarten'; cf. C. Nylander, *Ionians in Parsargadae* (1970), 114.
[73] Koldewey 1914, 127–8.
[74] Goetze 1946, 69 ll. 32–5, 71–2; cf. Langdon 1912, 138: 54ff.

baked bricks into the like(ness of) a mountain and built a large step-terraced *kummu (kummu gigunâtim rab[â])* structure as a royal abode for myself high up between the double walls of Babylon'.[74] Such a structure, comparable to that of the ziggurat (of which *gigunû/kukunnu* is sometimes a synonym) could well have been interpreted as a 'hanging garden'.[75] The extension made by Nebuchadrezzar of a high-platform for the so-called Principal Citadel on which he built his 'Northern Palace' has not been excavated at the Western river-side. Beneath it was a system of underground canals used for water-supply and drainage.[76] It is therefore possible that the royal gardens could have continued as terraces from the 'Northern Outwork' along the flank of this palace, which included the Museum,[77] and have looked out over the parkland on the northern flank of the new palace. Bergamini, with good reason, has shown that the *Östliche Ausfallwerk* was a reservoir or water clarification plant, forming part of the extensive water defence system, designed to act as a spill and to ensure continuous flow in the moat around the city to prevent silting.[78] This lay outside in the defensive moat wall built by Nebuchadrezzar in which the landing-stage steps provide an indication of the normal low-water level (−2.42 m.) just as the wear on the arches of the North Citadel drain vaults indicates the mean, normal and maximum levels, a difference of *c*.4 m. Babylon was completely surrounded by water. The later attribution of this phenomenon of the water defences was to the legendary Nitocris, but it is now known to have been the design of Nebuchadrezzar himself.[79] The location of the 'Hanging Gardens' here proposed (Plate I*b*) would accord both with the tradition and the practical convenience of such royal gardens as close to the private quarters of the palace and to water supplies, with access to the city walls and egress to more extensive parklands outside them where wild animals, including lions, were kept. There is, however, as yet, no direct reference to the latter in texts from

---

[75] CAD 5 (1956) 70.

[76] Bergamini 1977, 127, fig. 79.

[77] Unger 1931, 224–8; plan Tf. 36; G. Gossens, *RA* 42 (1948) 149–59.

[78] Bergamini 1977, 136–8.

[79] This is developed further in my article 'Royal and Temple Gardens in the Ancient Near East' in *Monarchies and Socio-Religious Traditions in the Ancient Near East* (Bulletin of the Middle Eastern Culture Centre in Japan No. 1 (1985) 37–43.

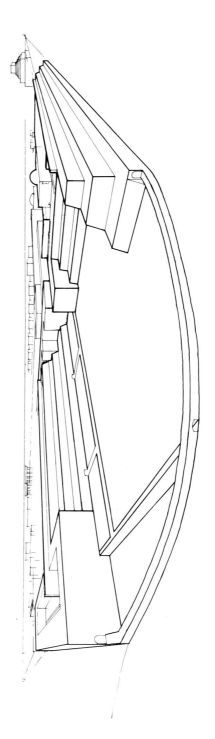

Fig. 7. Basic plan of the layout of the Royal Gardens of Babylon

Babylon.[80] Moreover, this proposed location is more appropriate than the usual supposition that the Hanging Gardens were above the so-called 'Vaulted Building', now known to have been store rooms with supporting buttresses for the Procession Way. Access to that site would have been through public quarters with a view overlooking the Ishtar Gate. In contrast the terrace gardens to the north-west of the citadel could have formed an amphitheatre-type construction overlooking the river and would have been a magnificent spectacle. (see pl. II, fig. 7)[81] They would have led through to the parks and gardens which surrounded the *akītu*-temple upstream outside the walls.[82]

There is then no reason to suppose that Nebuchadrezzar's royal garden was any less sumptuous than that of royal predecessors in Assyria, though perhaps with some variants due to climate. There Aššur-nāṣir-apli II (*c.* 876 B.C.) recorded that he planted gardens by the R. Tigris at Kalhu, watered by the Pati-nuhši canal from the L. Zab river, in which were all kinds of fruits and vines to provide temple offerings. 'From lands I travelled and hills I traversed the trees and seeds I had noticed I collected: cedar, cypress, box, *Juniperus oxcycedrus*, myrtle, *Juniperus dupracea*,[83] almond, date-palm, ebony, sissoo-tree,[84] olive, tamarind, oak, terebinth, *dukdu*–(nut), *Pistacia terebinthus*, myhrr-(type ash), *mehru*-fir, Dead Sea fruit(?), *ti'ātu*, Kanish-oak, willow, *ṣadānu*, pomegranate, plum, fir, *ingirašu*, pear, quince, fig, grape-vine, *angašu*-pear, *ṣumlalu*, *titip* (aromatic), *ṣarbutu*, accacia (?*zanzaliqu*), 'swamp-apple'-tree, *ricinus, nuhurtu, tazzinū, kanaktu* (an aromatic or frankincense?).[85] The canal waters came gushing down from above to the gardens; the paths (are full) of scent; the waterfalls (glisten) like the stars of heaven in the garden of pleasure. The pomegranate trees, which are cloaked with clusters of fruit like vines, enrich the breezes in the garden of (delight). (There) I, Aššur-nāṣir-apli gather fruit repeatedly in the garden of joys like

[80] The reading *an-ba-s*[i] in BIN I 23:16 is doubtful.

[81] Wiseman 1983, 140–1; Damerji 1981, 58–61 proposes a location on the west side of the Western Outwork but this would have been largely invisible to the Palace.

[82] Langdon 1912, 128 iv.11 (*ina kamāti*); 156 v 31; cf. *An.Or.* 9 (1937) 2 r.64; 3:44.

[83] cf. CAD 2 (1965) 328 sub *burāšu*; CAD 5 (1959) 189 sub *dupranu*.

[84] *BSOAS* 19 (1957) 317–8: *An.St.* 33 (1983), 70–1 for Dalbergia Sissoo Roxburg in Babylonia.

[85] The evidence points to a tree growing in mountains but capable of acclimatization in Assyria (CAD 8 (1971) 136).

an emaciated(?) person.'[86] Other texts attest the presence of
other trees there at this time, viz. medlar, elder, and other
fruit-bearing trees:[87] All these in season must have produced a
vista of colour and fragrance which added to the striking aspect
of the citadel.[88]

The Canals

As part of the rebuilding of the new palace area on the citadel
Nebuchadrezzar cleared and rebuilt the main canal (*nāru*),
Libil-hegalla 'bringer of plenty', long blocked with dust and silt.
Its level was raised while still allowing it to form the main drain
for the citadel with a grill and wooden spillway at the R.
Euphrates end.[89] This work necessitated the raising of the
Procession Street under which it flowed. Whether the canal's
alternate name was 'Royal Canal' (*nār šarri*)[90] is still uncertain as
is its precise eastward extension (*Libilhegalli palgi ṣît šamši*),[91]
which has been traditionally understood to flow into the Banītu-
canal with egress by the Zababa Gate.[92] It is equally not
impossible that so-called 'New Canal' (*nāru eššu*) to which the
texts refer in two ways as 'the upper New-Canal' and the 'Lower
New-Canal'[93] could be an alternate name for the Huduk[. . .]
canal running north of Etemenanki,[94] the 'lower' refering to its
course below the raised tell across the Eastern quarter of the city
(see Fig. 5). The location of the more than twenty named canals
in and around the city[95] is currently a subject being studied. Well
outside the main city defences upstream at Habl es-Sakr, *c.* 15
m. south-west of Baghdad, lies a 16 foot wide earth-core wall
faced on its north and south sides with a three-foot thick baked
brick wall bearing inscriptions of Nebuchadrezzar and overlaid

[86] Wiseman 1952, 33 ll. 40–8; cf. Postgate 1973, 239, but reading *pi-ia-q[i]* for pi-ia-z[i],
'mouse/squirrel?'; also ANET 559.
[87] Cf. Postgate 1973, 157 No. 240 5–6.
[88] Thureau-Dangin 1912, 223; Gen. 2: 8–9; Rev. 22:2.
[89] Langdon 1912, 89 Nr. 8 i.11–ii.1; cf. Berger 1973. 236–7.
[90] So RlA I 339a.
[91] Langdon 1912, 14 ii 7.
[92] Unger 1928, 338.
[93] Nemet-Nejat 1982, 446.
[94] Topography of Babylon v 60–1.
[95] Unger 1931, 94–107; cf. M.G. Ionides, *The Regime of the Rivers Euphrates and Tigris*
(1937) 74, 89.

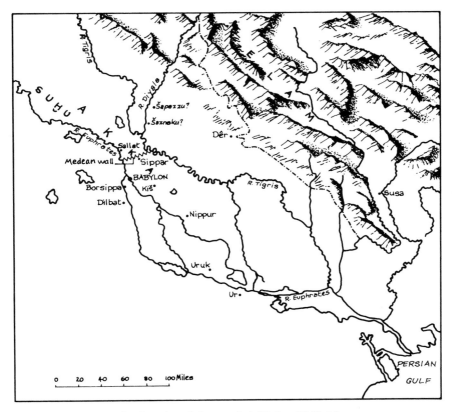

FIG. 8.   Location of the so-called 'Medean-Wall' defences

with bitumen. This has been traced for about ten miles.
Although the ends have not yet been found this may reasonably
be identified with the wall that the king claimed to have
constructed 'above Babylon from the bank of the river Tigris to
the bank of the river Euphrates' and thus with the 'Medean Wall'
described by Xenophon in 401 B.C. (see Fig. 8).[96] This would
also have provided a defence against nomadic incursions from
the north as had the earlier line of defences against the Amorites
in the time of Ibbi-Suen.[97] North of the wall was the old

[96] R.G. Killick, Preliminary report on Excavations at Habl es-Sakhr, (undertaken by Joint
British Archaeological Expedition to Iraq & Belgian Archaeological Mission Expedition 24
Oct.–14 Nov. 1983); 'Ancient Babylon's Median Wall', (Archaeology 3004), *The Illustrated
London News* (June, 1984), 77; to be published in H. Gasche and R.G. Killick, *Tell ed-Dēr IV*
(forthcoming).
[97] Barnett 1963, 19.

Assyrian province of Kar-Aššur which included part, at least, of the later district of Sin-Magir in which Opis is to be found.[98] This lay to the north of the Puqudu tribal lands and was *c.* 570 B.C. the territory of Nergal-šarra-uṣur.[99] Several tablets are dated at Opis (*Upia*) in Nebuchadrezzar's reign.[100] This siting of the northernmost defence wall for the Babylon area suits the operation by Cyrus when he diverted the R. Euphrates at such a distance as not to arouse immediate suspicion. This allowed the element of surprise for the attack on the city along the dried-up river and canal beds which gave access under and through walls into the citadel itself.[101]

The Streets

Nebuchadrezzar's repeated claim, substantiated by the associated building inscriptions recovered, was to have embellished the streets (*suqāti*) of Babylon, especially the Procession Way, the *mašdahu* i.e. the route along which the images of the gods Nabû and Marduk were drawn (Fig. 3).[102] This followed up the work of improvement undertaken by his father Nabopolassar but the roadway had sunk and needed a fill (*tamlû*) – a technique Nebuchadrezzar may have copied from Adad-šarra-uṣur's earlier work at Borsippa.[103] Since the fill was of 'clean earth' (*ina epirē^{hā} ella*) it would appear that the same care was taken in the work of the Sacred Way as was customary for the refounding of an older temple.[104] In conjunction with his work on the canal system he built a bridge where the Processional Way (*tallakti*) of Marduk crossed the new Libil-Hegalla canal. The Processional Way throughout its length was reinforced with burnt brick laid in bitumen, hardened with the insertion of limestone slabs and edged with durminabanda

---

[98] Von Voigtlander 1964, 126; S.J. Levy, *Sumer* 3 (1947) 5, 10 (i 27–iii 6). The later describes Nebuchadrezzar's works in the vicinity.

[99] Unger 1931, 285 iv. 42.

[100] E.g. Strassmaier 1889, Nos. 31, 322, 369, 419.

[101] Cyrus Cylinder (F.H. Weissbach, *Die Keilinschriften der Achameniden* (1911) No 2.

[102] For the order Nabû and Marduk (Langdon 1912, 196 29 2–5). This road from the Euphrates bank to Esagila was sometimes referred to as 'the procession road for the great son (of Marduk) Nabû (op. cit. 299 51:61 cf. 166 vi 61). Its northern part from Esagil to the Ishtar Gate being more commonly 'the Procession Way of Marduk'.

[103] Grayson 1975A, 75, n. on iii. 30.

[104] Langdon 1912, 29 4; cf. Ellis 1968, 15.

(breccia-type)-slabs. Thus the Processional Way – Ai-ibur-šabû, 'May the arrogant not flourish' – a title perhaps denoting its use for victory parades – was made into a raised highway (sulê).[105] At intervals between the Ishtar Gate and Esagil foundation boxes with inscriptions by Nebuchadrezzar commemorated this work.[106] The continuation of this road northwards to the akītu-house, and presumably even to the 'Summer Palace' (Bābīl) may have been designated 'the King's Highway'.[107] Nebuchadrezzar also restored Narrow Street (sūqu qatnu, sil.gig[nu]); earlier called sūqu kunuš kadru ('Bend-Down-Proud one')[108] because it led to 'the place where proud ones are compelled to submit', a description of Nebuchadrezzar's palace,[109] or from the river and place of judgement. The call which gave this name may have been proclaimed during ritual or penitential processions.[110] It may also be that 'Narrow Street' was partly arched, covered or with a low narrow gateway forcing the entrant to stoop. The location of the royal courthouse (bīt dīni ša šarri) in Babylon was in an area, presumably by the palace, accessible to the public.[111] The Babylon court-house, acting as a supreme court of appeal, is mentioned in several inscriptions.[112] Of the twenty-four streets including 'Carfax' (Crossroads), named in the Topography (ll. 63–85), only those associated with the major city gates can be orientated as yet, see Fig. 4. The economic texts provide us with additional street names, for example 'The street for the passing of joyous Nergal' (sūqu mūtaq Nergal ša hadê) and the 'Procession Street of Ṣarpanītu'.[113]

The Euphrates River Bridge

Access to the Procession Street from the river was by way of Nebuchadrezzar's strengthened landing stage, by pedestrian

---

[105] Langdon 1912, 88 ii 5–12; 198 Nr. 30.

[106] Al Kassar 1981.

[107] If it was not the name given to the route leading from the S. Palace and the abul šarri (King's Gate) along the R. Euphrates bank (harran kišad nāri, Nemet-Nejat 1982, 445).

[108] Unger 1931, 235:15.

[109] Langdon 1912, 94 iii 30.

[110] Lambert 1960, 560; cf. 3 R 66 i 28; KAR 214 i. 20.

[111] Lambert 1965, 5 iii.12.

[112] CT 22 105:26; YOS 7 31:9; TCL 13 222:5.

[113] Nemet-Nejat 1982, 87 (sūqu mūtaq [d]Nerga[l ša ha]dê); Langdon 1912, 282 viii.39 (mašdahu [d]Ṣarpānītu)

steps and by the bridge built with piers of limestone and brick shaped like pontoons pointing upstream (see Fig. 10).[114] Such a bridge was rare in Mesopotamia.[115] This appears to have been the work of Nabopolassar, completed by Nebuchadrezzar, which may have replaced an earlier pontoon bridge. Such a construction is depicted on Shalmaneser's bronze-gates at Balawat.[116] Later a gatehouse under the control of Guzanu, a Governor of Babylon, controlled the traffic.[117] The fee of 1 gur of barley for the passage of a ship[118] became, in the time of Darius, a *masīru*-toll extracted at a house at the head of the bridge and taken on boats moored at the bridge.[119] A half share of the of the income of the bridge belonged to the *šakin ṭeme* official of Babylon who rented out the right of collection at 15 silver shekels per month.[120]

The Temples

Nebuchadrezzar's main claim was to have made the cult-centre of Babylon a 'wonder'.[121] He continued his father's efforts on the embellishment of Marduk's temple Esagila and its subsidiary chapels. Much still required to be done following the vandalism of the ruthless destruction and desecration of the temple by Sennacherib which had made him infamous in 689 B.C.[122] Nebuchadrezzar worked on Marduk's chapel (Ekua), Nabû's main tample (Ezida), and the shrine of Ṣarpanītum adorning them within and overlaying them without with gold 'and made them to shine like a bright day'.[123] Emah, the temple of Bēlet-ilī was reinforced with brick work and the *kisû*-wall was filled with clean earth[124] providing a base for the rebuilding

[114] Wetzel 1930, 54–7; pl. 51; Bergamini 1977, 126 fig. 76.

[115] De Grave 1981, 146.

[116] L.W. King, *Bronze Reliefs from the Gates of Shalmaneser King of Assyria B.C. 860–825* (London 1915). pls. LXI–LXII; LXIV–LXV.

[117] De Grave 1981, 145; J.N. Strassmaier *Cambyses* 176:10.

[118] YOS 6 170:20.

[119] *Or* 35 (1966) 19; TCL 13 218:5.

[120] TCL 13 196:5; T.G. Pinches, *Inscribed Babylonian tablets in the possession of Sir Henry Peek, Bart.* (London 1888) No. 18; Strasmaier, *Darius* 64:1; 379:12.

[122] Langdon 1912, 7 ii.11 (*mahazi bābili^v ana tabrātim ušēpî*).

[122] Brinkman 1973, 94–5.

[123] Langdon 1912, 160 19 vii; 90 Nr. 9 i. 32. Such gilding of temples was not uncommon cf. 1 Kings 6:20–35; 7:48–51 (The first Jerusalem temple).

[124] Langdon 1912, 204 Nr. 43; 74 Nr. 1 ii 6; YOS 9 146.

needed following the depradations of Sennacherib who had claimed to have 'razed the brick and earthworks of the outer and inner (city)-wall, of the temples and of the ziggurat: and dumped these into the Arahtu. I dug canals through the middle of the city and overwhelmed it with water. I made its very foundations disappear and I destroyed it more completely than a devastating flood. So that it might be impossible in the future to recognise the site of the city and its temples, I utterly dissolved it with water and made it like inundated (land).'[125] This protection against the risen water-level by a kisû-wall and filling also enabled restoration work on the Temple of Ištar of Agade (é.maš.dari) to be undertaken. Recent re-excavation and partial restoration of this temple has shown the rebuilding work undertaken by both Nebuchadrezzar and Nabonidus and the care with which both recovered and followed the ancient foundation and lay-out (Pl. VIIIa).[126] This was a particular concern of both these kings[127] and a strong case can be made that the collection of 'antiquities', including inscriptions, housed in the 'Museum' in Nebuchadrezzar's North Palace was largely of his making with Nabonidus adding to it during his own restoration work in the capital.[128] Of the thirty-four objects found there nine could have been acquired as booty in Nabopolassar's or Nebuchadrezzar's early reign and thirteen of them discovered during the latter's excavation work in rebuilding the city. Four can be ascribed to possible discovery by Nabonidus and five to Darius I.

The recently discovered temple of Nabû-ša-harê with its doorway adjoining the Processional Way to its east shows another type of religious construction of the same period in well preserved mud brick. The floors and courtyard were bitumen covered and the shrine walls decorated with black and white geometric designs (Plates III a, b). The plan shows a typical *Breitraum* cella on the south side (See Fig. 9).[129] Since school

[125] Luckenbill 1924, 83:46–84:54; cf. Brinkman 1973, 94.

[126] Nasir 1979, 80–1 (on excavations in 1970, 1978–9).

[127] Ellis 1968, 13.

[128] Unger 1931, 224–8; RA 42 (1948) 149–59.

[129] The excavations are as yet unpublished (*Iraq* 43 (1981) 173). Reports were given to the Babylon Symposium in Baghdad 1979. For earlier references to this temple see Langdon 1912, 74 ii.7; called *bît harê* by Antigonus (Grayson 1975, 118 25). Langdon 1912, 106 (*bît nabû ša hariri*) is probably an ancient scribal error.

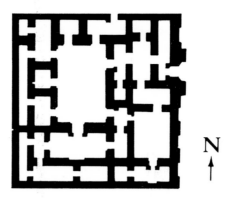

FIG. 9. Plan of the Nabû sǎ harê Temple

texts were found in fills it has been thought that the temple may
have functioned as a school or as a training place for priests.[130]

In addition Nebuchadrezzar worked on the city suburbs on
the West bank at Enamhe, Adad's temple in Kumar, and
Ekidurini (é.ki.tuš.kirzalla), the temple of Nin-eanna, in a
corner of the wall (ša tubqat dûri) in Babylon.[131] He also says he
was the first to have virtually rebuilt the temple of Ninkarrak
(Gula?) (Eharsag(il)), now rededicated to that goddess who had
granted him a successor (mušallimat per'īya), presumably to
acknowledge the birth of his son.[132] When it is remembered that
in addition to his claim to have undertaken building work on
sixteen temples in Babylon itself Nebuchadrezzar's texts allude
to work in twelve other cities, the extent of his operations can be
judged. That done at Borsippa as the hometown of Nabû was
considered also as part of 'Greater Babylon' and its outer defence
systems. There the Processional Way of Nabû was repaved with
stone blocks similar to those used for the same purpose in
Babylon itself.[133] The Ezida temple of Nabû was rebuilt on two
of its facades with a massive bonded wall around it.[134] The
temple itself was decorated with silver, gold and precious stones
and the corridors between the chapels and the walk-ways leading

[130] Cavigneaux 1981, 124.
[131] Langdon 1912, 75 No. 1. ii. 8–9.
[132] Berger 1973, 285–6 (Cyl. III 3 = Langdon 1912, 77 Nr. 1 iii 3–21); 104–8 lists the cities in
which Nebuchadrezzar carried out building works.
[133] Langdon 1912, 299 Nr. 52 3.
[134] ibid. & Nr. 50–1.

to the temple covered with clear glazed bricks.[135] Its massive
bronze threshold was inscribed with Nebuchadrezzar's names
and titles.[136] The cedar beams were overlaid with gold.[137]
Elsewhere in Borsippa he rebuilt the city wall (Ṭābi-supuršŭ)
and a quay-wall afforded it protection from outside. Also the
Etilla temple of Gula was rebuilt, as were other shrines and the
ziggurat.[138]

In all his restoration work in Babylon Nebuchadrezzar sought
to endow the temples with sumptuous and regular daily
offerings provided by a series of administrative measures making
demands on dependant groups and estates.[139] For the main
sanctuaries restored he claimed that provision came from his
own hand to load on the offering tables 'bulls, perfect specimen
of oxen, fine poultry, fish, birds including doves, honey, ghee,
milk, fine oil, beer, dates and fine wine' imported from the
north, the quantities being described as 'like river water'.[140] Such
offerings were listed in daily dated texts with the totals and name
of the agent given.[141] Collection-boxes (quppu) for public
offerings were also maintained.[142] Part of the latter was
presumably included in the issues of gold and silver to named
craftsmen to make rich garments and jewellery for the statues of
the gods and for the temple women.[143] Fine coloured wools were
issued for similar purposes.[144] Votive seals were presented to the
temple treasury by the king and others.[145] All this care lay behind
Nebuchadrezzar's repeated claim to be the 'Provider for (zānin)
Esagil and Ezida'.[146]

---

[135] ibid. 203 Nr. 42 4–5.
[136] *BM. Guide to the Assyrian and Babylonian Rooms* (1922) pl. XXIX; Berger 1973, 227.
[137] Langdon 1912, 72–4 Nr. 1 i.55–ii.5.
[138] ibid. 108 Nr. 13 ii 48–51; 98 No. 11 i.27–32.
[139] Lambert 1965, 6 iii. 19–20; Cavigneaux 1981, 118.
[140] Langdon 1912, 4 i 13–28; 90 i 24; 154 iv.52.
[141] For the early history of this literary type of offering list see *RA* 74 (1980) 59, No. 127; CT
44 71 (Sippar). Unpublished texts dated in the reign of Nebuchadrezzar include BM. 50832
(Access. Yr.); 50000 (1st); 49940 (2nd); 50155, 50757 (6th); 82562 (7th); 49892 (8th); 50615
(9th); 49488, 49956 (13th); 49489, 50022 (14th); 49935, 500064, 50492, 50735 (Yr. lost).
[142] Cf. Moore 1939, 57 (Eanna Neb. yr. 41).
[143] E.g. CT 55 (1981) 70, 837 (by hand of Nabû-bēl-šumāti in Nebuchadrezzar's 1st–24th
years; BM. 49471, 49621 (unpublished).
[144] Weisberg 1982, 218.
[145] Gibson 1977, 8: *JRAS* 1926, 446.
[146] Common on his brick inscriptions (Walker 1981, 71–91 Nos. 90–109).

The Ziggurat

In the days of Nebuchadrezzar the restored ancient temple-tower (*ziggurat*) named Etemenanki ('The Building which is the Foundation of Heaven and Earth') dominated the city. His father, Nabopolassar, claims that following the overthrow of the Assyrians he received a divine call to restore the sacred edifice which had been weakened and fallen. He was to make a new and firmer foundation 'on the heart of the nether-world'[147] (i.e. on a sunken platform) and to make its summit rival or equal the heavens.[148] To do this he called up diverse skilled labourers from all parts of his own country. They had to make bricks using picks, shovels or brick moulds of ivory and rare woods as Esarhaddon and others had done before in similar restoration work at Babylon.[149] This ceremonial included the laying out of the foundations and deposit-boxes, the king and his sons, including Nebuchadrezzar, taking part in the work. This may well have taken place early in his reign.

Nabopolassar had first rebuilt the river wall to the west and made an outer and inner supporting wall (*kisû*) which raised the enlarged platform by +3 to 3.50 m. above water level. Bergamini had shown from the recent Italian survey that this, with the increase in height of the base by Nebuchadrezzar to at least +4.80 m. along the west and north wall against potential flooding, proves that the lower stages and ascent stairs found by Koldewey in his deep sounding represent an earlier ziggurat, perhaps that of the Old Babylonian period. No bricks of the normal standard Nebuchadrezzar size (33 × 33 cms, Plate VIIIb) and none of his ziggurat-inscriptions were found in situ. It is also to be noted that that lower level ground plan and central stairway access does not align with Nebuchadrezzar's later reconstruction of the *peribolos* (Fig. 10).[150]

In undertaking his work on the temple-tower Nebuchadrezzar arranged for the traditional rituals by the *āšipu*- exorcists. He claims to have followed the wisdom given by the gods Ea and Marduk to build up the terrace to an overall height of thirty cubits. This was perhaps the height of building remains left by

---

[147] Unless *kigallu* here denotes 'fallow ground'.
[148] Langdon 1912, 62 i.44; 60 i 36; 94 iii 32.
[149] ibid. 60 i.32–iii.14; cf. Streck 1916, β. 9.
[150] Bergamini 1977, 140–50.

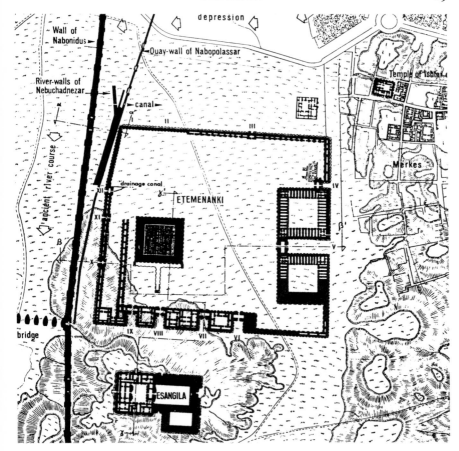

FIG. 10. The sacred precinct of the ziggurat (Etemenanki) and the Temple of Marduk (Esagila)

Esarhaddon's partial restoration. Nebuchadrezzar enlarged the temenos to the north and drained it off into the canal to the north and to the gateways of the temple platform. The work required the labour of many men imported from the lands he had conquered and he cited the kings who were made to carry the corveé basket, probably symbolicall̤, at the foundation laying ceremony. Chiefs and officials from the conquered territories as well as governors and chiefs of the Chaldean tribes and local people also participated. Babylonian officials from Hattu are said to have had great cedars of Lebanon brought to Babylon down the Euphrates for the work.[151] This massive

[151] Langdon 1912, 144 Nr. 17 i.3–iv. 4; 152 Nr. 19 iii. 19–iv.1.

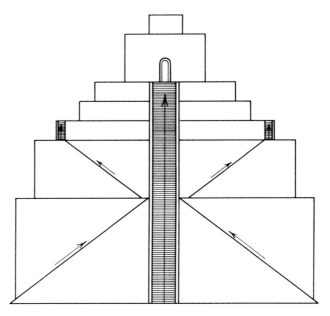

0 5 10 15 20 25 30 35 40 45 50 55 60   cubit (at c. 51 cm.)
0 ½ 1   2   3   4   5   large measure (at c. 6.10 cm.)

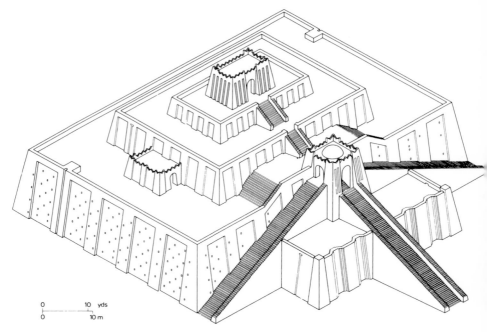

0   10 yds
0   10 m

Fig. 11. Suggested reconstruction of the ziggurat
a) W. von Soden
b) Ziggurat of Ur-Nammu at Ur

undertaking took many years to complete, as Nebuchadrezzar repeatedly claims it had done. The final work on the filled-in terrace (*tamlû*) and the cladding of the upper-dwelling of Marduk with blue-glazed enamelled bricks made the topmost stage look like the heavens themselves.[152] The topping-out was marked by joy and rejoicing.[153]

The difficulty in reconstructing the ziggurat is largely due to its thorough destruction following the undermining of the temenos by later flooding. Xerxes' deliberate act of breaching the Euphrates River bank may have led to a temporary change in that river's bed to flow between the citadel and Etemenanki. Alexander removed such upper debris as remained, carting it off together with any of Nebuchadrezzar's inscriptions there may have been, to leave a clear base for his own planned rebuilding of the ziggurat.

The so-called 'Esagil tablet', now in the Musée du Louvre (AO.6555), remains the best source for the dimensions of the temple-tower[154] with its height equal to its base (i.e. 15 × 15 (× 15) GAR = c. 90 × 90 (× 90) m).[155] Though dated Seleucid Era 83 (229 B.C.) the tablet appears to be a copy of an older original, perhaps made to aid the restoration planned by some successor of Alexander. Many different proposals for a plan based on this text have been made all assuming that the traditional architectural form was followed (Fig. 11).[156] This was of seven stages including the upper temple, though Nabonidus at Ur c. 550 B.C. adopted a seven storey style in keeping with economy and more southerly traditions (Plate IV; cf. Fig. 11b).[157] A tablet from Babylon, perhaps a school copy of the 'ideal plan', was made 'according to the tradition of Nabû-šuma-iškun of the lineage of Ah'ūtu' (BM. 38217).[158] If not a mere exercise, this may be the plan of a smaller scale ziggurat for Anšar (also a title of Marduk). Ah'ūtu may reasonably be dated to the first half of the seventh century B.C. (Fig. 12).[159]

---

[152] ibid. 114 Nr. 14 i.38; 98 Nr. 11 i.23; 126 Nr. 15 iii.15.

[153] ibid 90 Nr. 9 i.39.

[154] AO.6555; Unger 1931, 239.

[155] 1 GAR = 5.94m. For full bibliography and discussion see Parrot 1949, 22–8.

[156] See Von Soden 1971, 260.

[157] C.L. Woolley, *The Ziggurat and its Surroundings (Ur Excavations* V, 1939) 125–43, pl. 86.

[158] BM. 38217; Wiseman 1972, 141–5 & Fig. 2.

[159] H.M. Kummel, *Familie, Beruf und Amt im spätbabylonischen Uruk* (1979) 109 & n.9; 141 n.246.

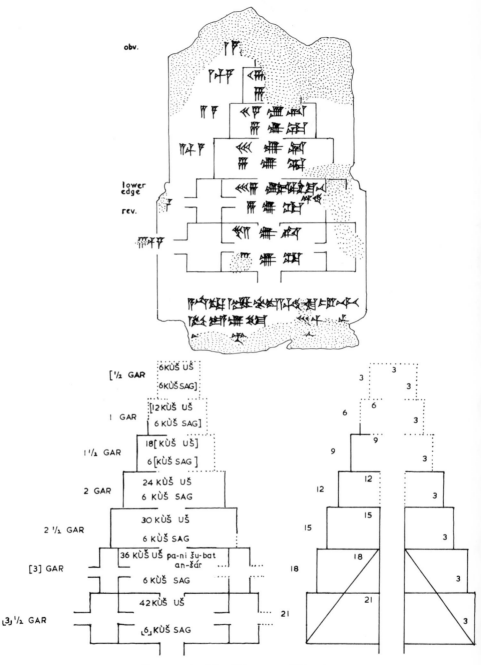

obv.

lower
edge

rev.

['½ GAR] 6 KÙŠ UŠ
          6 KÙŠ SAG]

1 GAR   [12 KÙŠ UŠ
          6 KÙŠ SAG]

1 ½ GAR 18 [KÙŠ UŠ]
          6 [KÙŠ SAG]

2 GAR   24 KÙŠ UŠ
          6 KÙŠ SAG

2 ½ GAR 30 KÙŠ UŠ
          6 KÙŠ SAG

[3] GAR 36 KÙŠ UŠ pa-ni šu-bat
          an-šár ....
          6 KÙŠ SAG

          42 KÙŠ UŠ
[3] ½ GAR ₍6₎ KÙŠ SAG

FIG. 12. a)   The Aḫ'ūtu text (BM. 38217)
(above)   copy of cuneiform text
(left)   Transliteration, showing measurements by cubit (kùš) of length (uš), height
(sag) and width (1 gar = 12 kùš)
(right)   Measurements in metres (depth – width – height) and reconstruction showing
access

Nebuchadrezzar followed the dimensions of the earlier foundation which, as excavated by Koldewey, dates to about the Old Babylonian period and equals the scale of the Esagila tablet. That had a triple access stairway on the south side but its orientation differed slightly from that taken by Nebuchadrezzar to accommodate to his new temenos.[160] Discussion continues as to the precise form of access. Herodotus implies that 'the ascent to the upper (levels) was made on the outside, round all the towers'[181] and this may well be correct for the uppermost stages. It is likely that the roof of the upper temple, gained by a staircase inside according to a text detailing that structure, was for the purposes of astronomical observations.[161] On the basis of the Esagila and Ah'ūtu texts a reconstruction of the ziggurat of Nebuchadrezzar's day may be proposed. (See *frontispiece* and Fig. 13; cf. Plate IV and Figs. 11a and 12.)

The 'Court List'

A prism found in the western extension of Nebuchadrezzar's new palace commences with a summary of his building operations in different parts of the country and in Babylon itself.[162] It continues with a list of small quantities of supplies presented to Esagil. These are too small to be part of a great popular celebration such as was customary at the opening ceremony of a major building project. Such feasts are recorded on the completion of Aššur-nāṣir-apli II's work at Kalhu c. 876 B.C., of Sennacherib's building at Nineveh,[163] and earlier that of Solomon at the dedication of the temple and palace at Jerusalem.[164] The quantities may therefore simply refer to a special donation to the temple of Marduk to celebrate the opening of Nebuchadrezzar's new palace c. 570 B.C., since that building is the last item listed in the prologue.

The remaining columns of the text continue with a list of

[160] Bergamini 1977, 139–41, pl. I.
[161] Cf. Von Soden 1971, 260 Abt.1; Ravn 1942, pls. XIV–XV. For the astronomical observations reported to Assyrian kings in the preceding century from Babylon, Borsippa, Uruk, and rarely Dilbat, see Oppenheim 1969, 122; cf. Strabo *Geog.* 16 1.16; Pliny *Nat. Hist.* VI. 121ff.
[162] VAT 7834 (Istanbul); Unger 1931, 282–94.
[163] Wiseman 1952, 28; Luckenbill 1924, 116 viii 65–76; 125 49–51.
[164] 1 Kings 8:63–6.

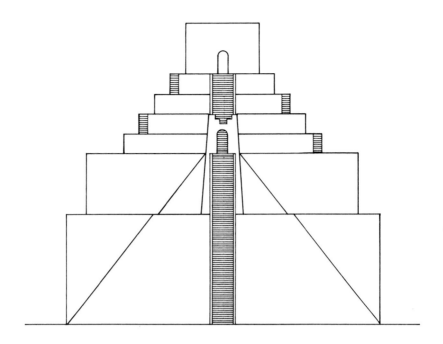

FIG. 13. New proposal for reconstruction of the Babylon ziggurat

personal names and the appointments held. It has therefore
been taken to be a list of officials at the court of
Nebuchadrezzar.[165] Against this is the absence of offices and
names known from other texts[166] and the inclusion of officials
from districts far from the capital. The text lists those stationed
around the king (*manzāzu ša rēšiya ušaṣbit*, iii 34). First a
group of at least nine high-officials (*mašennu*), of these Nabû-
zēr-iddinam the 'Chancellor' or 'chief baker' (*rab nuhatimmu*) is
to be identified with Nabuzaradan (*rab ṭabbāhîm*)[167] present at
the final seige of Jerusalem (Jer. 39:9–10). The list continues
with Nabû-zēr-ibni the chief of the *kāṣiru* (craftsmen or low-
ranking) officials; Erib–[. . .] in charge of palace officials;

---

[165] ANET (1950) 307–8.

[166] E.g. Nergal-šarra-uṣur and other officials named in Jer. 39:3; no secretary-scribes of high
military office holders are included.

[167] cf. Kinnier Wilson 1972, 80.

Sīn-šar-ilāni the major domo and five others. These are followed
by Ardiya the *mašennu* of the queen's household and Bēl-uballiṭ
her scribe, then by the Chief of Protocol Silla and Nabû-aha-uṣur
the chief of the engineers (*rab kallāpi*), four men in charge of
female employees (*amēlāti*), Nabû-zēr-ibni the cup-bearer,
Nergal-rēṣūa the chief of the singers, Ardi-Nabû the archivist of
the crown-prince,[168] Ea-idannu the chief-*pū'ma*, Nabû-mār-
šarri-uṣur in charge of mariners and Hanunu, president of the
royal merchants.

The following section of the list names eleven senior officials
(gal.meš) who acted as district officials of Babylonia, most
simply designated by their tribal association, Sin-Magir,
Tupliaš, Puqudu, Dakkuru, Gambulu, Amuqu. A few have
their specific office stated, e.g. the governors (*šaknu*) of the
Sea-land and of Yaptiru, the district-governor of Sumandar and
the 'true governor' of Zame. One, Nādin-ahi, is the Iú.é.maš[169]
of Dēr and so may be a lesser official representing or acting for
that city. The district and local governorships shown here
indicate that Nebuchadrezzar was continuing the arrangements
long in use in Babylonia though with added sub-divisions
perhaps due to the increased population.[170] The governors are
followed by the names of nine officials (*qēpu*) appointed to
oversee designated towns. The text ends with a list, regretably
broken, of the kings of Tyre, Gaza, Sidon, Arvad, Ashdod and
Mir [. . .] without their personal names. (v. 23–29). The length
of columns on the prism would allow for only another six kings
to be cited, insufficient for the text to have included the kings of
all the places conquered or controlled by Nebuchadrezzar. The
whole would therefore seem to be a document drawn up to
record a procession to commemorate a special occasion. The
inclusion of the kings of Tyre and Sidon may indicate their
presence as new tribute-bearers. The absence of Yaūkin
(Jehoiachin) of Judah, Aga' of Ashkelon and an (unnamed) king
of Lydia known to be in Babylon may suggest that their names
have been lost in the break.[171]

---

[168] *sipiru*; cf. BASOR 93 (1944) 15 n.6.

[169] lú.é.maš/kid is taken by R. Borger, *Assyrisch-babylonische Zeichenliste* (1978) No. 324 as
šangû, 'Priester', but the context seems to require a high state or tribal official Cf. N.Bab en.é.

[170] J.A. Brinkman, 'Provincial Administration in Babylonia under the Second Dynasty of Isin',
JESHO 6 (1963) 233–42.

[171] Weidner 1939, 925–6, 928, 934.

The Labour Force

Nebuchadrezzar makes frequent reference to his acquisition of massive tribute (*biltu kabittu*) including prisoners from his campaigns,[172] while the Old Testament makes specific allusions to the deportation of skilled and other labourers. The 10,000 taken from Judah in his eighth year were stated to be 'officers and fighting men and all the craftsmen and artisans' (2 Kings 24:14) included both in this general number and in the more specific (because counted?) numbers of 3023, 832 and 745 persons listed for the seventh, eighth and twenty-third years (Jeremiah 52:28–30).[173] Some of these would have been required to devote their skills to building-projects in progress in Babylon. In doing this Nebuchadrezzar was but following a practice common in Assyria whereby foreign personnel were employed on rebuilding the capital; 17,500 from Bīt-Adini alone by Shalmaneser III at Assur and 47,074 by Aššur-nāṣir-apli II at Kalhu among them.[174] The texts refer to such persons as 'exiles' or 'deportees' (*galîtu*).[175] In Assyria, on completion of their building chores, the 'prisoners' were sent off to other places of residence, some allotted to governors or officials, to army personnel or a few to the temple administrative services.[176] The Neo-Babylonian texts indicate a tendency for the authorities to settle together groups of exiles who originated in one or more adjacent area. Most of this evidence comes from Nippur in the following century and, if not due to the mere archaeological 'accident' of discovery, this may show a special policy. Nippur played little political part in Nebuchadrezzar's day and was controlled by officials from Babylon.[177] Thus Lydians and Phrygians around Nippur lived in one *hadru*–community and Urartians and Melideans in another. Bīt-Ṣurraya may be another *hadru* for Tyrians in Nippur.[178] Similarly, if Chebar and Tel Abib of Ezekiel[179] are correctly equated with the *nār kabāri* near

[172] Grayson 1975, BM. 21946 13, 17, r.4′, 13′ 24′.
[173] Malamat 1968, 154–5.
[174] Oded 1979, 55–8.
[175] *galītu, šaglūti, ulteglū (galû* cf. Heb. *galâ). Ittekir*, to be alienated from homeland, is also used. See also Zadok 1977, 14.
[176] Oded 1979, 112–5.
[177] Zadok 1978A, 274, 326.
[178] Zadok 1978, 60–1.
[179] Ezekiel 1:3; 3:15; Ezra 2:59.

Nippur this could be an indication that the Judeans were exiled there also under similar arrangements. The Išqillunu (Ashkelon) settlement by the Sin-Magir canal at Nippur and place-names implying groups of Greeks and men from Gaza could indicate a similar situation. More than eighty-nine settlements along sixty named canals in the Nippur region are known. With this concentration of foreigners can be compared the use of Nippur in Middle Babylonian times as a place for groups of forced labourers including prisoners of war and others from as far afield as Syria and Elam.[180] Sidonians appear to have been settled at Uruk (c. 580/579 B.C.), perhaps as nearer the Persian Gulf. Above Sippar the Dūr-kurašu village on the R. Euphrates was a place where men from Hatti-land were congregated either in a labour or military cantonment.[181]

There is no evidence how 'prisoners of war' were treated at the time though selected highly skilled foreigners were respected and given rations from the royal palace. Those listed in texts c. 572 B.C. found in the 'vaulted building' of the Southern Citadel received oil and barley. They included 'Salamyâma a gardener' and Gadi'il probably Judeans.[182] Carpenters or woodworkers (naggārē) from Byblos[183] and Arvad[184] were particularly noted and named, presumably for their potential skills. One hundred and twenty-six men from Tyre who were shipwrights or mariners (malāhhē) were granted rations of $\frac{1}{2}$ sila of (sesame) oil, that is the same as given to three mariners from Ashkelon and the royal princes from Judah held in Babylon.[185] This may show that, though not personally named, they were engaged in directing the construction of a fleet of ships to counter Necho II's Red Sea navy. These vessels, according to Herodotus, were to be floated down the R. Euphrates to a new port Nebuchadrezzar established at Teredon.[186] In a similar manner Sennacherib had built ships in Nineveh which, when manned by men from Tyre, Sidon and Cyprus, were dragged overland from the R. Tigris to R. Euphrates at Opis and then floated

[180] C.B.F. Walker, An.St. 30 (1980) 5–22; JCS 32 (1980) 20–2.
[181] Gadd 1958, 85 n.1. (Nabonidus Chronicle ii 13).
[182] Weidner 1939, 927; cf. Shelemiah, Jer. 36: 14, 26; Gadi'il (cf. Num. 13:10).
[183] ibid. 929.
[184] ibid. (B ii 43; D 16).
[185] Weidner 1939, 930–2 (A.190B).
[186] Katzenstein 1973, 321f.

down to the Persian Gulf.[187] Egyptians given rations while on
watch at the boat house (*bīt sapānatu*) and at the *qēpu*– official's
office (*bīt qēpūti*) may have been involved in this also. The use
of *sapānatu* implies a decked ocean going vessel.[188] The presence
of Egyptians in Babylon would not have been strange since they
are named as there at this time and earlier in what must have
been a somewhat cosmopolitan community.[189] Royal ration
texts refer also to eight Ionian carpenters (*naggārē* ^meš ^amēl
yamanāya) and shipwrights. Since the latter are named it may
be assumed that they were not hostages or common prisoners of
war but specially skilled craftsmen.[190] It has been suggested that
their names, Kunzumpiya, Labbunu, Aziāk and Patam, look
very un-Greek and they may be Anatolians.[191]

The 713 Elamites who were also given rations in Babylon[192]
Von Voigtlander thinks to have been taken in the brush with
Elam in 597. Their numbers are, however, large for a group in
detention in the capital itself and Elam may here refer to a
location on the Khuzistan border of the Persian Gulf.[193] The
mention of Nabû-lē'u (pa.da?) who was over (*eli*), not simply in
charge of (*ina qāt*), Elam in 592 B.C. might mean that he was
appointed to control regional affairs[194] rather than relate to a
group of south Elamites in Babylon perhaps also engaged in
ship-building.

'The privileged City'

The need to employ foreign unskilled labour in the
reconstruction of Babylon could result from manpower
shortages for such a massive project and from the need to
dislocate the country's normal economy as little as possible while
the work was in progress. It could also have been required by
the time-honoured special status of the citizens of Babylon itself.
From at least the Kassite period the citizens there had been

---

[187] Luckenbill 1924, 73 58–64.
[188] Barnett 1958, 229.
[189] Wiseman 1966, 156.
[190] Cf. Weidner 1939, 932–3.
[191] Braun 1982, 23.
[192] Weidner 1939, 929–30 (B r ii 7, 13–14).
[193] Von Voigtlander 1964, 117.
[194] Weidner 1939, 930 (B r. ii.15).

granted *kidinnu* rights. These exempted them from call up for corvée or military duties, from certain taxes and from imprisonment.[195] Babylon was 'a city of (protected by) *kidinnu*' (*āl kidinni*).[196] This appears to have been reaffirmed by Adad-šuma-uṣur when he was allowed to enter Esagila *c.* 1195 B.C.[197] Brinkman has shown that it was a major concern of Assyrian kings following Shalmaneser III to regrant and maintain this status to Babylon and Borsippa and occasionally to Sippar and Nippur. This was done with drink and bread, that is by a ratified covenant-treaty given to the citizens with splendid garments and other gifts.[198] These *kidinnu*–recipients are described as 'freed (of burdens) by the great gods' (*šubarrē (ša) ilāni rabûti*).[199] Tiglath-pileser III had reaffirmed the *kidinnu* of Babylon[200] and Sargon II, Esarhaddon and Ashurbanipal expressly continued it, as they did for their Assyrian temple-city of Assur. Sargon stresses how he made up for an earlier period when Babylon had been deprived of these concessions.[201] He says that at Assur his intention, in addition to the normal benefits and exemption from trade-tax (*mikis kāri*), was that 'they might walk about in Ešarra before him (the god) in order to preserve (the cult?).'[202] The expressions *mahar ili ittalluku* and *aršu balaṭ [libbišunu?]* would seem to refer to the service of the gods. Since Marduk-apla-iddina II and Sin-šarra-iškun had preserved the same privileges for Babylon it would be surprising if Nebuchadrezzar had not done so also. The terms of the *kidinnu* could be varied and needed to be conferred anew in explicit terms by each monarch. The use of exiles in the construction work in the city would thus have enabled Nebuchadrezzar to avoid any infringement of the rights granted to leading families on whom he counted for support. This was important in a complex and volatile tribal situation in the region.

Exile, and the conditions it imposed, would always have been in the minds of subordinate people, for mass deportation was a

[195] Brinkman 1979, 228; Reviv 1983.
[196] Borger 1956, 21 Ep. 23:18.
[197] Grayson 1975A, 70 ii.27.
[198] *WO* 4 (1967) 32–3 vi.4.
[199] YOS 1 38 ii.28; Reviv 1985, 7, 12.
[200] *Iraq* 17 (1955) 23–5; Brinkman 1979, 236–7.
[201] *Iraq* 7 (1940) 86 l.1.
[202] *Iraq* 37 (1975) 16 l. 37.

constant threat to the smaller nations by their more powerful neighbours.[203] Any major infringement of treaty or loyalty-oaths carried with it the prospect of exile for king, royal family, officials and people who 'will not return to his country and not see his country again!'[204] On these grounds many West Semites had found themselves exiles in Assyria.[205] While the threat, and practice, was used to subdue rebel peoples,[206] it also served to repopulate ruined or abandoned regions.[207] There is no evidence that following employment on royal building enterprises[208] the men were used in labour gangs *in perpetuo*, nor were such captives normally made slaves.[209] Nebuchadrezzar appears to have used his deportees, including Jews, in a similar way. Some, as others who had faced such hardship before them, are attested as rising to professional status and owning land and vineyards in the land of their sojourn.

This survey of activity in Babylon has sought to present a view of it as rebuilt by Nebuchadrezzar to be a major international and local administrative centre. The palaces and shrines were grandly ornamented to be a wonder for all people to behold. The temples were enlarged and adorned to make the place a 'holy city'. Such is the background to the exile of the Jews whose skills had played some part in recreating this metropolis. They on their part longed for their own temple, city and freedom and saw about them a glory which they believed to be transient.

---

[203] Oded 1979, 43–5; 54–5; Kitchen 1970, 5.
[204] ANET (1969) 532 (Treaty of Mati'el-Aššur-nērari V); Wiseman 1958, 51 ll. 291–5.
[205] Malamat 1971, 1074–6.
[206] Borger 1956, 25 Ep. 37:12–24.
[207] ABL 942; deportees to Babylonia settled in Til-Karmi (P. Rost, *Die Keilschrifttexte Tiglat-Pilesers III* (1893) 26 l. 149); cf. Judaeans placed in Til-Abib (Ezek. 3:15).
[208] Oded 1979, 58 (Arabs at Nineveh).
[209] Cf. *JNES* 32 (1973) 90; Oded 1979, 72–3.
[210] Zadok 1977; cf. Rab-Shakeh's promise in 2 Kings 18:32.

III

SOME BIBLICAL AND OTHER TRADITIONS

While Nebuchadrezzar was rebuilding the great city of Babylon and adorning it with the tribute extracted from the territories he now dominated, his concern was that the city should regain its place as the cultural centre of the ancient Near East. One way of achieving this was by training selected foreigners in the whole range of Babylonian science which was itself an expression of the local philosophy and wisdom. The extension of Babylonian civilization had influenced courts and learned circles far afield over almost three millennia.

Diplomatic hostages

At the highest level members of the royal families from nations who had been overrun, or were still hostile, were treated with special attention. They received rations from the king's palace in Babylon itself. Texts from the Southern Palace show that in 592/1–569/8 Nebuchadrezzar granted Jehoiachin of Judah (*Yaukīn šar* ^{māt} *Yaudaya*) oil from the royal stores.[1] Supplies were granted also to his five sons[2] who were in the care of a Babylonian appointee one Qana'ama, possibly a Jew (Qana-yaw).[3] This may indicate that the family as a whole was held not merely as royal hostages to be displayed on state occasions but to be trained for eventual return to their land as loyal supporters of the Babylonian regîme. This practice had been followed earlier by Ashurbanipal with Elam and it is of interest that the leader of the Jewish exiles returning home from Babylon c. 538/7 B.C. under Cyrus' decree was a grandson of Jehoiachin bearing the Babylonian name Zēr-bābili (Zerubbabel).[4] The use of the title 'King of the Judeans' in these

---

[1] Weidner 1938, 925–6 (B ii. 38–40; C ii. 10–11, 17–18; D 20–1.) On the name Yau'kīn see also *BASOR* 216 (1974), 5–7 (*Yaw*); cf *VT* 28 (1978), 113–118, 29 (1979), 87–97.

[2] Cf. 1 Chron. 3–17 (presumably later, seven sons).

[3] Zadok 1979, 8, 38.

[4] Ezra 2:2; 3:2; cf. 1 Chron. 3:19.

ration texts whenever the Babylonians list Jehoiachin, who had been taken prisoner traditionally in fetters, could mean more than that this was his title when captured five or more years earlier. For much of his time in Babylon (from 587 B.C.) his successor Zedekiah, a Babylonian nominee, lay blinded in some adjacent prison in the same city. Thus Jehoiachin was probably regarded as no more than just the titular head of the Jewish diaspora in Babylonia. He may have been held in the hope of some eventual change of loyalty which would have allowed him a resumed rôle as client-king in Judah but this never happened and he remained a 'king in captivity', though his 'royal' status while in Babylon has been questioned by Avigad.[5]

However, Jehoiachin maintained an assistant (*n'r ywkn*) in Judah named Eliakim who sealed transactions in Tell Beit Mirsim, Beth-Shemesh and Ramat Rahel with an inscribed seal bearing his and Jehoiachin's name. These royal estates may have been among those deliberately left in Judah to supply the Babylonian occupation forces with wine.[6] During Zedekiah-Mattaniah's reign in Jerusalem as 'ruler' (lugal = *šarru/mlk*) it may have been considered by the Babylonians that Jehoiachin was *de jure* king of Judah.[7] The Judeans themselves traditionally considered him their king though in captivity for thirty-seven years until, at the age of fifty-five,[8] he was released by Nebuchadrezzar's successor Amēl-Marduk on 24 March 560 B.C. (2 Kings 25:27). He was then given as a favour a higher status than other kings who were 'eating regularly at the king's table' in Babylon. The expression 'to eat at the king's table' is explained as the receipt of regular royal allowances (v. 30). These were usually of barley and oil and occasionally, meat, ointment and clothing. They were handed by the administration to a dependant and not necessarily consumed in the palace itself.[9] In the second millennium such royal favours were widespread and promulgated by royal edict. The benefits could include a house and land sufficient for the maintenance of the

[5] N. Avigad in F.M. Cross (et.al.ed.), *The Mighty Acts of God: In Memoriam G.E. Wright* (1976) 298f.; cf. Malamat 1973, 213.

[6] *JBL* 5 (1932), 77–103; 16 (1943), 66 n.9; *BA* 5 (1942), 50–1; See also p. 38 and n.260. D. Ussishkin, *BASOR* 223 (1976) 1–5 argues for an earlier date for the *n'r ywkn* stamps.

[7] Wiseman 1956, 73, l. 13.

[8] cf. 2 Kings 24:8.

[9] *Kurummat šarri* (CAD 8 573, 576 for refs.).

whole family.[10] For the non-hostage recipient certain duties were attached to the status thus conferred.[11] The privilege of 'eating at the king's table' was also granted to selected officials.[12] In all cases it implied loyalty to the donor.

In addition to royal hostages certain skilled foreign craftsmen were fed in this way. The Babylonian ration texts of 592 B.C. list with the two sons of Aga', king of Ashkelon, under the supervision of Halabizu, 3 mariners, 8 officials (sag) and an unspecified number of musicians (*nârē*) from the same city.[13] At the same time rations were issued to Egyptian shipwrights and to specifically named Egyptian officials. The inclusion of personal names suggests that these were more than mere prisoners-of-war. One, Harmaṣu,[14] like another Egyptian Nikû (Necho) in the same text, was responsible for the safe delivery of supplies (^{amēl} *mandidu*), rather than of information (*mandētu*). They, like the Egyptians named in a broken text dated in Nebuchadrezzar's third year,[15] were in Babylon before the major contest with Egypt in 601 B.C.[16] Other Egyptians named include Uhpar'asā, the *šušān*-official in charge of horse-grooms,[17] and Pusumeski, the *šušān*-official in charge of monkeys (*uqupē*).[18] The latter, like the performing bears, jugglers, acrobats, snake charmers and others presumably formed part of the royal court entertainment.[19]

The presence of 'refugees' at the Babylonian court is also seen in the lists of those given rations by the palace. The only named Mede, Kurbannu, and a Lydian Urkula are so described (*maqtu*).[20] There is no reason to believe that in Nebuchadrezzar's reign either of these lands were under his

---

[10] cf. 1 Kings 11:18–19.

[11] CT 22: 150:120; CAD 8 576; cf. Glaeseman 1978.

[12] CT 22: 150: 20; cf. 1 Kings 4:27; Neh. 5:17).

[13] Weidner 1939, 928 (B.r. 6, 8; C r. ii. 22; D 25).

[14] Wiseman 1966, 155; *RlAA* 433; The Har[maṣu] of BM. 57337, 7 could read Har[maki] = Eg. Harmachis (suggested to me by E. Edel in 1967).

[15] Wiseman 1966, 156, BM. 78177, 7 (CT 44 89). Other persons named Miṣirāya, 'the Egyptian', are known from Babylonia at this time; for Egyptians in Assyria see *An. St.* 30 (1980), 72.

[16] Lipiński 1972, 235.

[17] Weidner 1939, C i. 9.

[18] Weidner 1939, 930–2 (A17, r. 20–3; C i. 9–15); cf. *JAOS* 73 (1953), 154; 74 (1954), 12, n.21. On long-tailed Rhesus macaque monkeys imported from India into Babylonia see *An.St.* 33 (1983) 81–3.

[19] *St. Or.* 46 (1976), 60–1; cf. 1 Kings 10:22.

[20] Weidner 1939, 930 (C i. 23), 934 (C i. 24).

control unless the statement of the extent of his dominion in the west as 'conquering from Egypt to the city of Hume, the city of Piriddu and the city of Lydia (^{al}lu-u-du)' implies this and is not just a statement of general boundary lines.[21] At all periods of Mesopotamian history kings gave support to those of influence who disagreed with a government hostile to them, but these 'refugees' were from countries with whom Babylon had treaty relations. Some may have returned later to their own country in alliance and good will with their benefactor. Nebuchadrezzar would have been well aware of the danger of harbouring dissidents. When the Assyrians had given refuge in Nineveh to the sons of Urtaki who had been driven from Elam by a usurper Tept-Humban (*Teuman*), it became a *casus belli* when Ashurbanipal refused their extradition. After he had defeated the Elamite attackers two members of Urtaki's family, Humbanigaš II and Tammaritu II, were given parts of Elam to rule as client-kings of Assyria. The Babylonians may have continued to use this technique, to judge from the title 'king' assigned to named foreigners in both the 'Court List' and the Weidner ration lists.[22]

Foreign Trainees

Nebuchadrezzar appears to have made a deliberate policy of re-educating foreigners with a view to their use in their own homeland or in the Babylonian internal administration. The tradition preserved in Daniel 1 implies that the selection was made by royal order to the most senior court official (*rab sārîsîm*). This Aramaic title, the Babylonian *rab ša rēši*, was also common in the Assyrian court where the Aramaic *rbsrs* stands for the Akkadian *rab ša rēši*.[23] Such officials held the equivalent status of 'governor' (*šaknu*) and there is no unequivocable evidence that they were usually, or necessarily, eunuchs.[24] The Babylonian official who removed Jeremiah from prison was of this class (Jer 39:13) and may have been thus specially qualified to deal with foreigners. Ashpenaz (Dan 1:3

[21] Lambert 1965, 7 l. 21.
[22] See pp. 81.
[23] BM. 81–2–4, 147 (unpublished).
[24] *JAOS* 87 (1967), 523; Kinnier Wilson 1972, 47. S. Parpola *OLZ* 74 (1979) col. 33 considers them eunuchs in every case.

'ašp^enaz) may have been a non-Babylonian, to judge by his name, though for his court duties he would have had a Babylonian name as did the official holding this position in Nebuchadrezzar's so-called 'Court' list.[25]

The king of Babylon's directive was clear;

i. to select young men of good appearance, physique and intelligence from the ranks of royal or noble families (part^emîm, cf. Esther 1:3; 6:9).

ii. Since they were to enter the royal service ('to be stationed in the royal palace'), and possibly the wider civil administration, their existing abilities were important if they were to be able to grasp the whole range of Babylonian education. The course was to last three years – normally that for a competent scribe – and to cover 'the language and literature of the Babylonians' (Dan. 1:4).

iii. Those selected were given palace rations at a high level (Dan 1:5 pat̲ bag, 'rich food').[26] The Judeans' objection to this was not to the source, since even the plainer diet would mark their indebtedness and obligation to the king, so much as to its nature. There is no indication that food from the royal table had previously been offered to idols.

iv. The men chosen were given new official names. The meanings of these, and indeed whether they were originally Babylonian or Aramaic, is uncertain (Dan 1:7). Berger has recently considered the name Belteshazzar given to Daniel as a rendering of Bēlet-šar(ra)-uṣur, 'O lady (Ištar) protect the king', rather than of the generally accepted abbreviation from (Marduk)-balaṭsu-uṣur, 'May (Marduk) protect his life.' He also suggests that Shadrak, Hananiah's name, could be šadurāku, 'I am very much afraid', but the expected Babylonian form would be šūdurāku. Mishael, renamed Meshach, could be mēšāku, 'I am insignificant' or mešāhu, 'I am forgiven'.[27] However, Nebuchadrezzar's more frequent use of mêsu/mēsu, 'to crush, squash' would make the rendering 'I am crushed'; but these latter suggestions produce a personal name of a

---

[25] Unger 1931, 285 iii. 38–9.

[26] Gk potibazis, 'dainties'; but this is probably Aramaic rather than O. Persian (cf. Kassite bagur(r)u).

[27] Berger 1975, 225–33; Millard 1977, 72, E. Lipiński, VT 28 (1978), 233–5 rejects the Old Persian etymologies on which Berger draws. Cf. CAD 10/2, 42.

type unlikely to have been conferred on someone due to
stand in the royal presence. Azariah's court name,
Abednego, has been taken to be an Aramaic form of
Ebed(Arad)-negû, the latter element a play on Nabû,
'servant of the shining one'.[28]

The City of Learning

Babylon would have prided itself on being the 'city of wisdom'
(*āl 'nēmeqi*)[29] a title held earlier by Assur when capital of
Assyria.[30] At this time it was unique to Babylon and the ability to
learn such wisdom was expressed in the epithet 'master of
wisdom' (*āhiz nēmeqi*) borne by the Neo-Babylonian dynasty.[31]
A striking characteristic of scribal schools at Babylon, occurring
more frequently there than elsewhere at centres of learning in
Babylonia, or indeed earlier in the Assyrian capitals, was the use
of the colophon on 'literary' texts (e.g. gabari *bābili*). The
tradition continued at least until the first century B.C. in
Babylon and also in Uruk. Sufficient texts have survived to show
that schools in Babylon in Nebuchadrezzar's reign continued to
copy certain sign lists and the series har.ra=*hubullu* with its
word lists, paradigms and extracts of legal terminology. Other
text copies at this time include religious documents of all kinds,
the Epic of Creation,[33] Gilgamesh,[34] the origin of kingship,[35] the
legend of Anzû,[36] fables[37] and omens of various categories
including those about devils and evil spirits (*utukki lemnūti*)[38] as
well as texts of possible historical interest.[39]

It is noteworthy that in Nebuchadrezzar's Nabû ša harê

[28] Berger 1975, 226; or *negû* 'to sing joyously', used of Babylon and Marduk in *Emuma eliš* vi, 73; vii, 179, but not known in a personal name.

[29] The claim would be based on the attribute of Marduk 'the god who created all the skills required to make civilisation' (*ilu bān nēmeqi*; Langdon 1912, 216 ii. 4).

[30] Thureau-Dangin 1912, 201.113, Wiseman 1952, 34, 103 for Kalhu).

[31] Berger 1973, 73.

[32] Hunger 1968, 157 and No. 420; i.e. at least seven texts from Babylon are so described in heir colophons to every one from Ashur, Nineveh and Kalbu; KAR 144 r. 17.

[33] Labat 1935, 18; BM. 33851 etc.

[34] E.g. CT 46, 17–35 (late Babylonian); BM. 33538 (unpublished).

[35] BM. 46565.

[36] *JCS* 31 (1979) 65 (YBC 9842); BM. 36708, 40217, 40975 (unpublished).

[37] The *duqduqqu* – bird fable was copied at Babylon as late as 242 SE (70/69 B.C.); CT 52 98.

[38] *JCS* 39 (1979), 216, 218–19.

[39] E.g. BM. 33340; copy of Adad-apla-iddina accounts.

temple almost a thousand tablets were discovered recently. Most were in fills under the staircase of Room 7, others in Rooms 3, 4 and 15, probably reused as building materials by later occupants. The majority of the texts were Neo-Babylonian school texts ranging from large to small in size and from elementary exercises to advanced groups of Akkadian verbs, lists of personal and divine names, with citations and quotations from letters and from earlier writings. Although most bear colophons, these are not dated. Cavigneaux considers the tablets, as the excavator does the temple, to date to the early Neo-Babylonian period. The form of the colophons is another indication of their local origin which is confirmed by the discovery of two tablets in a kiln in the south-west corner of Room 15. The texts represent the first stages in a scribe's education undertaken in what may have been a school on an upper floor or nearby, though there is no further indication that the temple itself served this rôle. The colophons show that students dedicated their finished products or examination exercises to the god Nabû, sometimes with a prayer added: 'O tablet speak for me before the god', or 'May Nabû make my mind more enlightened'. Another was written 'to prolong days, to avoid sickness, to attain material and spiritual well-being and to increase understanding.' There is a prayer for longer life so that the student may develop his (cuneiform) signs and write his tables better.[40] The names of the students making such dedications have an added interest in that some could have been the contemporaries of Daniel and his companions. However, in view of their exclusive way of life and distinctive beliefs the Judeans would presumably not have so placed their work in a pagan temple (cf. Dan. 1:8, 17).

The Babylon Literary Traditions

The Daniel narrative refers to the expatriate scholars having 'knowledge and understanding of all kinds of literature and learning' and to Daniel himself as able to 'understand visions and dreams of all kinds' Dan 1:17) – the latter a special branch of Babylonian learning. The background to such statements is furnished by a comparison with Babylonian literary and omen

---

[40] Cavigneaux 1979; Khalil 1981, 36.

texts extant in, and sometimes dated or datable to, Nebuchadrezzar's day. Despite the growing influence of Aramaic and the consequent bilingualism and biscripturation sufficient cuneiform texts survive to show the continuance of the older literary traditions. The complete series har.ra = *hubullu*;[41] the series har.gud[42] and diri[43] and a range of proverbs are included.[44] Copies of the laws of Hammurapi from the Old Babylonian period,[45] of Adad-apla-iddina's accounts[46] and a Hittite hymn to Ishtar were now made.[47] Nabopolassar had the royal ceremonies of Uruk copied as an aid to re-establishing the ritual in Babylon and this example Nebuchadrezzar seems to have followed. The absence of some genres, among texts known from the early part of the Chaldean dynasty may be the result of archaeological accident, or due to failure to publish texts in museum collections, rather than simply their non-existence.

An on-going tradition for which Babylon was later to be remembered was that of its 'astrologers'. The Chaldean astrologers in Babylon lived in a special city-quarter and were distinguished from the tribe of the same name settled by the Persian Gulf. Oppenheim has shown that this class of experts was grouped into academies or teams of ten or more scholars who, at Babylon, played a significant rôle in the observance of lunar, solar and stellar phenomena and advised the Assyrian king on the political and religious significance of such matters. Their reports were more frequent and more detailed than those of the contemporary Assyrian scholars, especially those at Assur, who adopted a similar system and acted primarily as the transmitters of this Babylonian science there.[48] These reports depended on meticulous and regular observation of astronomical data. This was done both for the astrological series *Enuma Anu Enlil*, copied in this reign, and for the type of text now called 'astronomical diaries.' These diaries may well have been

[41] MSL I–XIV; cf. BM. 33885–9; 84466 (bilingual).

[42] BM. 40760 (unpublished).

[43] BM. 33708, 40481 (unpublished).

[44] Lambert 1960, 275 (for the ongoing tradition); BM. 38282, 38486, 38539, 38596, etc. (unpublished).

[45] Wiseman 1962 (BM. 47859).

[46] BM. 33340 (unpublished).

[47] *JCS* 21 (1967), 255–7.

[48] B.L. van der Waerden, 'Chaldäer' in *Sitzungsberichte der Heidelberger Akad. d. Wissenschaften, Math.-Naturwiss. Klasse* 1972, 197–227; Oppenheim 1969, 103, 115.

collected systematically from the time of Nabû-nāṣir (*c.* 740 B.C.) to whose reign the cycles of periodic intercalation in the calendar go back,[49] but the earliest diary yet identified in this reign comes from Nebuchadrezzar's thirty-eighth year.[50] Since this type of text is also known from the reign of Nabonidus[51] there is no reason to doubt that this practice was well established at Babylon and continued the observations which had earlier served the Assyrian court. Each of these texts, of which almost a thousand come uniquely from Babylon, covers half a year with a section devoted to observations of at least the major planets and metereological information for each month. The latter shows that the weather at Babylon has not changed basically over the last two thousand five hundred years. Detailed observations of Venus and of consecutive lunar eclipses arranged in 18-year groups have survived for the years 608/7. 591/0–572/1; 589–573 B.C. and been included in texts copied in Nebuchadrezzar's day.[52] This continuity of record led to the development of Goal Year texts giving lunar position in relation to normal stars – later used to predict planetary and lunar phenomena for a given year. Similar developments led to Almanacs devoted to recording planetary positions, lunar and solar eclipses. Ephemerides texts enabled the place of any heavenly body to be found for a given time and thus the prediction of the new moon and its last visibility and eclipses followed. This legacy of Babylon was to have a profound influence on Greek astronomy and, through later Arabic sources also, on modern astronomical and nautical tables.[53]

Mathematical tables and algebraic texts as well as problems and solutions in geometry were mainly related to the astronomical sciences. Tablets giving weights and measures could have been in the minds of, or available for reference to, those 'wise men of Babylon' who sought to read 'the writing of heaven' (*šiṭir šamē*)[54] which they took to be the mysterious writing of the wall of the main hall in the Southern Palace used

---

[49] Parker 1956, 1; BM. 33809 (unpublished list of intercalated vi 1/2).

[50] Sachs 1974, 48 (–651); *AfO* 16 (1953), Tf. XVII (after p. 424); Sachs 1955, xii, No. 160 (months I–III, X–XII; 567–566 B.C.).

[51] BM. 37456 (unpublished).

[52] Sachs 1955, Nos 1386, 1419.

[53] Sachs 1948, 271–90.

[54] Gadd 1948, 93–5.

by Belshazzar in October 539 B.C. (Dan. 5:26–8). The phrase *m^{e}nē' m^{e}nē' t^{e}qēl uparsîn* had as its most obvious rendering 'mina, mina, shekel and half-shekel (i.e. 60:60:1:½ (shekel)). This must have baffled the astrologers since it was not obviously linked to any recognisable name of a king or of his successors, the usual subject of such writings.[55] Nor did it relate to the series of omens expressed in numbers like that compiled for a son of Ashurbanipal and copied in Babylon. That series gives predictions, including length of reign or other event relating to an individual, with its most frequent allusion to 'the king of Babylonia (Akkad)'.[56] It is a late seventh century application of astronomical and mathematical data which, by two centuries at the latest, was to become renowned as Babylonian horoscopy.[57] Another development beginning now was the transition from planetary to zodiacal astrology which was sometimes considered to have an influence on medicine,[58] much as it was also then thought did the weather.[59]

The astronomical diaries add the current price of staple commodities such as barley, dates, wool and sesame-oil against the silver shekel. Where prices fluctuated during the month the fact is stated. The recorded height of the river Euphrates is given and many of the diaries close with noteworthy political, secular and temple happenings known to the scribe and introduced by *alteme* – 'I heard'. Most of the historical notices which ended the diaries survive only for the Seleucid period and, when published, will provide a unique glimpse of the continuity of worship at Babylon even after the foundation of Seleucia.[60] All these details imply the maintenance of regular daily records at Babylon which formed the basis of the reliable and objective Babylonian Chronicle.[61] Abstracts from this source were used for different purposes such as historiography, historical enquiry and comparative studies.

---

[55] Cf. Luckenbill 1924, 94 l. 64; 103, ll. 27–9 for Nineveh as 'city built on earth in imitation of a heavenly prototype.' The Khorsabad 'constellation inscription' on the palace wall is interpreted as a symbolic writing of the name Bēl-harran-bēl-uṣur, son of Sargon II.

[56] Gadd 1967, 55–8.

[57] Sachs 1952, 49–75.

[58] *JA* 244 (1956), 275–80.

[59] *ZA* 66 (1976), 235–6.

[60] Pinches 1902, 483–4 (=BM. 34050, 45693 unpublished). The death of the late Professor A.J. Sachs will regretably further delay publication.

The amassing of economic data in official texts, excerpted in Chronicles of Market Prices,[62] may have been used for checking values in such cases as fines imposed as legal penalties in contracts. A few scholars believe that the record in equivalence of silver may be an early indication of the advent of a money economy.[63] There is no undue indication of inflation during Nebuchadrezzar's rule, though it has been suggested that the subsequent 50% rise in the decade following his death was due to the drain on military and manpower resources demanded by Nebuchadrezzar's unceasing activity in the field and in the reconstruction of Babylon. There is, however, no evidence that normal canal clearance declined, though the closure of some trade routes and famine, combined with some lack of firmness in central control after his death, may have led to a steady inflation of 200% in 560–485 B.C. in an often changing political situation, which brought Nebuchadrezzar's 'empire' to an end.[64] Nabonidus at 'Teima', if there for economic purposes, could only stem this trend a little. Comparison with the texts before Nabopolassar seized power shows the price of corn in Nebuchadrezzar's early reign at c. 180 sila per shekel.[65] This compares with 40 sila per shekel under Šamaš-šum-ukin at a time of severe economic crisis, and with 234 sila per shekel under Ashurbanipal.[66] The rental of a large house in Babylon was half a shekel (12 loaves of bread (akalu) daily for four years) in Nebuchadrezzar's 22nd year.[67]

The absence of certain genres of literature has already been noted but their presence may be implied on other grounds. Some earlier traditional texts may have been reinterpreted. For example the series lugal.e, a term formerly used as an epithet for Babylonian kings, seems to have now been reinterpreted by taking e as a geographical name referring to Babylon in the first year of Nebuchadrezzar and soon thereafter the series became

[61] Wiseman 1956, 4–5; Grayson 1975, 8.

[62] Grayson 1975, 60–2, 178–9; Chronicle 23 selects prices over at least seven hundred years (7–10) and adds years without a reason given, so l. 13 is taken to be the ninth year of Nebuchadr[ezzar I]. Such chronicles or lists of prices were continued in Neo- and Late Babylonian texts (e.g. BM. 34479, 45724 etc. unpublished lists of prices).

[63] AJES 33 (1974), 17.

[64] Contra Saggs 1962, 17.

[65] Cf. B. Meissner, Warenpreise in Babylonien (1936), 5.

[66] Zawadzki 1979, 183–4.

[67] Dougherty 1923, No. 35.

extinct.[68] Since proverbs were copied, as they and tables were in the later Seleucid period in Babylonia, it is reasonable to assume that the associated proverb-riddles were also. Daniel's stated ability to solve them (5:12) would be real and not necessarily a mere reflection of the inclusion of this art in court training under Mesopotamian influence which had reached as far as Jerusalem in Solomon's day.[69]

Dreams

A few fragments of texts related to the Assyrian Dream Book have survived in the Neo-Babylonian script and the whole tradition could thus have been studied and used then.[70] Dreams and their interpretation play a major part in the Daniel story (1:17; 2; 4:18–27) though there, as elsewhere in the Old Testament, the emphasis is on the piety and sagacity of the God-inspired interpreter. This culminated in Daniel's supreme achievement of interpreting a dream which the dreamer himself had forgotten. This was done with the help of another divinely given vision. The dreams from this period employ symbols taken from life not fantasy.[71] One such indirect method of interpretation is recorded in the seventh year of Nabonidus when an astrologer reported a dream in which he saw the Great Star, Venus, Sirius, the sun and the moon and foretold he would be able to interpret it as a favourable omen for the king and his crown-prince Belshazzar. This he did satisfactorily two days later.[72] In another dream Nabonidus saw his 'royal predecessor Nebuchadrezzar and an attendant standing in a chariot. The attendant said to Nebuchadrezzar, "Do speak to Nabonidus so that he can report to you the dream he has seen!" Nebuchadrezzar heard him and said to me: "Tell me what good (signs) you have seen." I answered him: "In my dream I beheld with joy the Great Star, the moon and Jupiter (Marduk) high in the sky and it called me by my name."'[73] Such dreams within a dream occur in the Dream Book (Tablet X), 'if he has seen a

[68] Brinkman 1968, 167 and n.1021–2.
[69] JNWSL 5 (1977), 81.
[70] E.g. BM. 79–7–8, 77.
[71] Oppenheim 1956, 209–10.
[72] YOS 1 (1915), 55, No 39; Oppenheim 1956, 205.
[73] Langdon 1911, 278 (vi 4–36); ANET (1969), 310.

dream within a dream and reported the dream . . .'[74] This is paralleled in the Babylonian Talmud which states that such a dream within a dream will be fulfilled.[75] Nabonidus also claims to have received an order from the god Shamash to rebuild his temple in Sippar 'in a dream which I had and which (other) people had also'.[76] This presumably implies confirmation of the dream by others. While the interpretation of the dreams in the book of Daniel is not the present concern it must be noted that the interpretations proposed by modern commentators vary considerably.

Apocalyptic

Associated with visions and dreams to depict the future is that of apocalyptic, a literary genre formally presented as the work of Daniel in a Neo-Babylonian setting. Apocalyptic is commonly associated with, and usually dependent on, prophecy.[77] The idea that such apocalyptic writing, with its dualism in which good will outweigh evil, originated in a later Zoroastrianism needs review. Boyce now believes that Zarathushtra lived and taught well before the ninth century B.C. and the conflict between good and evil and 'angelology' are found in demonstrably pre-sixth century Mesopotamian and Hebrew literature.[78] The element of 'predictive prophecy' is found in Assyrian documents though usually interpreted there as *vacinia ex eventu*.[79] There they are without any suggestion of a climactic end to world history.[80] These texts have justly been compared with Daniel 8:22–25: 11:3–45. They are couched in astronomical terminology, show some connection with astrology, and are considered by some as only 'a type of prophecy (which) is simply a literary creation without reference to specific historical events.'[81] The symbolism of coming world history shown as four succeeding powers is most clearly given in Nebuchadrezzar's

---

[74] *KAR* 252 iii 59–60; K. 4103, 9'–10'.
[75] *Berakoth* 55b; Oppenheim 1956, 305 n.229.
[76] CT 34 28:67.
[77] Lambert 1978, 1–7.
[78] M. Boyce, *A History of Zoroastrianism* (Handbuch der Orientalistik I viii 2A) I (1975), 190–1 (1700 BC); II (1982), 3 ('before 1200 BC); *BSOAS* 47 (1984), 75.
[80] Grayson 1975A, 21; Hallo 1966, 231ff.; Dan 1:27, 29; 10:14 refers only to 'one day in the future'.
[81] Biggs 1967, 128;

vision of a large awesome statue and in its interpretation in
Daniel 2:31–45:

'The head of the statue was made of pure gold, its chest and
arms of silver, its belly and thighs of bronze its legs of iron, its
feet partly of iron and partly baked clay.' (Dan. 2:32, NIV).

Destruction occurred in the reverse order, the head being
identified with Nebuchadrezzar (Dan 2:38) and the other parts
as succeeding kingdoms usually interpreted as Babylonia –
Medes (Persians) – Greece – Rome. However, since all parts
were broken to pieces at the same time (v. 35), one interpreter
considers the image as a symbolic review of the Assyrian dynasty
as Nebuchadrezzar concerned himself with the problem of the
succession![82] Swain has argued that the division of history into
four empires and a fifth to follow was already known in Rome by
the time of Aemilius Sura (187–171 B.C.), but others oppose
this view. The representation of four metallic ages goes back at
least to Hesiod's *Work and Days* of the seventh century B.C.[84]
Passages in Zoroastrian texts, though known only at present
through an A.D. 6th century Pahlavi text, are thought to be
based on a lost Avestan account of Zarathushtra's vision of a tree
with four branches made of gold, silver, steel and 'mixed iron'
respectively which he interpreted as covering human history.[85]
All these sources imply a long history of the tradition and it is
not possible to say that Daniel is dependent on any one of them
even if he was not the originator of a four kingdom sequence in
depicting world history. It must be observed that the Book of
Daniel adopts a precise annalistic style characteristic of several
Babylonian literary forms:

'A mighty king will appear, who will rule with great power
and do as he pleases. After he has appeared, his empire will be
broken up and parcelled out to the four winds of heaven. It will
not go to his descendants, nor will it have the power he
exercised, because his empire will be uprooted and given to
others' (Dan 2:3–4). Such wording is deliberately open to
diverse interpretations and applications.

Comparison is made with the more detailed type of text

[82] Löwinger 1947.
[83] Swain 1940, 9.
[84] P. Walcot, *Hesiod and The Near East* (Cardiff, 1966), 85–6.
[85] Lambert 1978, 8 (with variant of seven branches).

composed in the seventh century B.C. in a 'prophecy' series from Assur each section of which begins, 'a prince will arise and rule x years.' From the length of reign given, and sometimes other supporting data, it is generally possible to identify the unnamed kings, in this instance as the four kings of Babylon who reigned some five centuries earlier (*c.* 1175–1057 B.C.).[86] But such interpretations are by no means sure. A Seleucid period library text copy made for an astrologer in Uruk, but which appears to have been composed much earlier, reads:

'After him a king will arise but he will not judge the judgement of the land or give decisions for the land but he will rule the four world regions and at his name all the world (–regions) will tremble. But after him a king will arise in Uruk who will make judgements (provide justice) in the land and make decisions for the land. He will confirm the rites of the cult of Anu in Uruk. He will remove the protective deity (*lamassu*) of Uruk from Babylon and let her dwell in her own sanctuary in Uruk. He will renew Uruk. Uruk's gates he will rebuild of lapis lazuli . . . He will fill the rivers and fields with abundant yield. After him a son will arise as king in Uruk and become master of the four world regions. He will exercise lordship and kingship in Uruk (tir.an.na.ki) until his dynasty is established for ever. The kings of Uruk will exercise rulership like gods.'[87]

Interpretations differ as to the identity of all the unnamed kings involved here but there is general agreement that the last two good kings were Nabopolassar and his son Nebuchadrezzar.[88] If so, it accords with their known close association with that city. The allusion to their ruling 'like (as if they were) gods' would give added point to the emphasis placed by Daniel on the supremacy of God as the Most High Sovereign over the kingdoms of men. (4:17, 25, 32, 34, 37).

A fragment of a Dynastic Prophecy published by Grayson describes in prophetic terms the rise and fall of dynasties (or empires?) from the fall of Assyria through the rise and fall of Babylonia and of Persia to the rise of the Hellenistic rulers. The first column is damaged and broken and originally may have covered the end of Assyrian domination in Babylon and the rise

---

[86] Ibid., 10.

[87] Hunger 1975, 371–2; (my translation).

[88] Hunger 1975, 374: Lambert 1978, 11–12.

of the Chaldean dynasty there.[89] Though Grayson interprets the damaged section which followed a missing introduction (i. 1–6) as characteristic of Nabopolassar, the statements are general. There is a reference to Nippur, bringing booty into Babylon, the refurbishing(?) of Esagila and Ezida and the building of the palace in Babylon. This section (i. 15–25) could apply also to Nebuchadrezzar and part of his reign and that of Amēl-Marduk continued on the upper part of col. ii, now missing, for when the text becomes legible again (ii 4′–10′) it concerns Neriglissar and Labashi-Marduk. In these and the succeeding prophecies no names of kings are given though their identity is again sure from the circumstantial details. No reign was omitted if it is assumed that the fragment comes from an originally six-column tablet.[90] The accuracy of the historical content has not been questioned apart from the unexpected reference to what seems to be a defeat of the Greek army (*sukuptu ummāni hanī i*-[. . .] which would be surprising in the light of the known victory of Alexander at Gaugamela (near Kirkuk) at this time.[91] In the text paragraphs are introduced by the prophetic formula previously used in the late Assyrian period:

'A re(bel) prince will arise and (will establish) the dynasty of Harran. For seventeen years (he will exercise sovereignty). He will oppress the land and will (. . .) the festival(?) of Esagil. (He will build) a wall in Babylon and will plot against Babylonia (Akkad).' (ii.11–16).

'A king of Elam will attack (and take the sce)ptre (?). He will summon him from his throne and (. . .) He will seize the throne and the king who left the throne (. . .). The king of Elam will change his place and settle him in another land (. . .). The king will take strong action against the land(s) and all the lands (will bring in) tribute. During his reign Babylonia (Akkad) will (be) a peaceful abode.' (ii. 11–24)[92] These sections clearly refer to Nabonidus and Cyrus.

Most assume a late Hellenistic date for the Daniel tradition and consider the Jewish work to be dependant on these later sources. However, this has not yet been established beyond

[89] Grayson 1975A, 24–37.
[90] Lambert 1978, 13.
[91] Grayson 1975A, 26; 34, iii 17; cf. Wiseman 1977, 335–6. See also p. 118.
[92] Grayson 1964, 14.

question and has to be examined in the light of the evidence of a literary genre the elements of which are found before the sixth century B.C. It must be emphasised that in its scale the Daniel apocalyptic is unique and is couched in such a way that the historical symbols and allusions may, probably deliberately, be open to many and varied interpretations as history has shown.

Any estimate of literary influence is difficult to judge in a period when insufficient texts have survived to enable a precise line of transmission to be traced. While the few Jews at the royal court might have been subject to such influence through their retraining, those named in Daniel appear to have passed their careers within the establishment at Babylon. According to the Daniel narratives they reacted against the philosophical and religious bases which permeated Babylonian culture and literature. However, there is no indication of their rejection of Babylonian learning as such, but rather of their reinterpretation of it in the light of their own traditional religious thought. Lambert has examined the texts of periods in which such Babylonian influence has been postulated, including that of the exile, and has argued for a far earlier date, such as the Amarna period, when it might have had an effect on Old Testament literature and traditions.[93] Where there was contact between courts at an international level concepts peculiar to the one were transmitted through diplomats, experts or merchants.

It has been questioned whether it was feasible for foreigners to have ready access to the king in person as reflected in the book of Daniel. The picture given by the Assyrian texts of the previous century is one of court-officials of every level, and even private citizens, asking that 'the king may give attention to his servant' (ABL 1285). To call the king's notice to a case or to request an audience of him was 'to speak the word of the king' (*amat šarri qabû zakāru*). It was also possible to write letters of appeal to the king, though these are largely concerned with matters of land-tenure and most cases would have been dealt with in the active local district courts set up by Nebuchadrezzar, renowned as 'the just king' (*šar mēšari*). The *kidinnu*–right allowed citizens of Babylon to have their cases tried by the king himself.[94]

[93] Lambert 1979, 67–9.
[94] Postgate 1975, 419–20.

Daniel and his companions could have been well known to the king from his personal choice and investigation of them before they were granted official and permanent posts in the palace (Dan. 1:19–21). Daniel at least would have had a right of entry to give information to the king, primarily on matters of omen-interpretation and perhaps on Judean affairs. This right would have been the more readily used after his promotion to 'chief of the astrologers and ruler of the judicial districts' (*mᵉdînâ*) of Babylon (Dan. 2:48; 4:9). Similarly foreigners contributing to an international interpretation of events had found a ready audience at the royal court as earlier had Jonah at Nineveh[95] and later the astrologers, possibly from Babylon, at Herod's palace in Jerusalem.[96]

Daniel's length of service of about sixty years (602–539 B.C.)[97] can be compared with that of several of the 2997 scribes mentioned in the Babylonian texts of the first millenium. 1263 of these scribes worked in Babylon; 548 in the reign of Nebuchadrezzar. Some, according to Dandemayev, lived to seventy or eighty years of age or more. For example, Nabūahhē-iddin appears as a scribe and witness in texts dated 590–547 B.C. and slaves who survived to between fifty and eighty years of age are known from dated transactions in which their names are given.[98]

Nebuchadrezzar's Character

Although the Old Testament remains a primary source for any intimate understanding of the character of the Babylonian king something can be gleaned from the Neo-Babylonian texts. His royal inscriptions are marked by an absence of war-like stances and, despite their reuse of paleo-Babylonian traditional epithets, they emphasise 'moral' qualities.[99] Some texts follow the ancient tradition of using the first person (*anāku*) which does not of itself necessarily denote a bombastic egocentricity.[100]

[95] Wiseman 1979, 44; G.M. Landes, *Eretz Israel* 16 (1982), 147–70 dates the book to the sixth century.
[96] Matthew 2:1–7.
[97] Dan. 1:3; 8:1; 10:1 *c.*602–539 B.C.
[98] Dandamayev 1980, 184; 1982B 36.
[99] Garelli 1981, 5.
[100] Cf. S. Smith, *Statue of Idrimi* (1949), 14 1.1; and Nebuchadrezzar *passim* (S. Langdon 1912, 70 No. 1 i 10 etc.).

Thus Nebuchadrezzar's statement: 'Is not this the great Babylon *I* have built as my royal residence, by my mighty power and for the glory of my majesty?' (Dan. 4:30) must be interpreted in the light of other characteristic statements.

Nebuchadrezzar, like his contemporary Jeremiah (1:4), claimed a divine vocation as did most kings of ancient Mesopotamia and wrote: 'After the lord, my divine begetter, made me, Marduk had my form built within my mother. When I was born and created I continually sought the guidance of the gods and always followed the way of the gods (*alakti ilē*). I continually paid attention to the artistic activities of Marduk, the great lord and the god who made me . . . Without you, my lord, what exists? You establish the reputation (lit., make straight his name) of the king whom you love, whose name you pronounce and who pleases you. You make his reputation one of justice and set a straightforward course for him. I am the prince who obeys you, the creation of your hand. You begot me and entrusted me with the rule over all peoples. According to your graciousness, O lord, you who watches over them all, lead them to love your exalted lordship. Make the fear of your godhead be in my heart. Prolong (the days of) the one who pleases you, for you truly are my life!'[101]

Allowing for the formal language and traditional phraseology used, Nebuchadrezzar, having made such a public and written pronouncement, would be bound to follow the ceremonial rituals prescribed by the Esagil temple authorities. This would include the consultation of omens and the 'astrologers' before any major occasion or decision of state. No king would have undertaken a military campaign without doing so, especially if the war was thought to be in response to the attack of an enemy. Copies of the Babylonian war ritual held at Esagil had been sought by Ashurbanipal for his own library[102] and another was made from an inscribed writing-board (*lē'u*) at Babylon by Nabû-zēra-iddina the chief lamentation priest at Harran.[103] Similar rituals continued to be copied in Uruk later.[104]

In a description he gives of injustice abounding in the land,

---

[101] Langdon 1912, 122–4, No. 15 (i. 23–32, 55–ii.1). Sheriffs 1976, 239–40.
[102] *CT* 22, 1.
[103] Elat 1982, 6, 15.
[104] Hunger 1976, No. 12.

Nebuchadrezzar paints a scene reminiscent of the classic Sumerian reformer Urukagina and of earlier Babylonian kings and rulers of Judah:

'The strong used to plunder the weak who was not equal to a lawsuit. The rich used to take the property of the poor. Regent and prince would not take the part of the cripple and widow before the judge, and if they came before the judge he would not preside over their case. Even if the judge took a bribe or present he would pay no attention to it (the case); if they did not accept any decision from him . . .' In contrast, Nebuchadrezzar claims that 'he was not negligent in the matter of true and righteous judgement, he did not rest night or day, but with counsel and deliberation he persisted in writing down judgements and decisions arranged to be pleasing to the great lord Marduk and for the betterment of all the peoples and the settling of the land of Babylonia (Akkad). He drew up improved regulations for the city and rebuilt the law-courts. . . .' Three examples of his judgement follow: the first of a criminal who had been executed and his head displayed as a deterrent throughout the land (vi. 17–19). To perpetuate the effect a stone replica of the head was fixed above the outer gate of the courts for all to see. It was inscribed with a warning against reopening a case in which judgement had been delivered and sealed.

Nebuchadrezzar claims to have prohibited the use of bribery, bringing a sense of satisfaction to the land to which he brought stability and peace. No one was to be allowed to intimidate the people. The second instance given was of a false charge of murder which led to the accuser and accused being subject to the river ordeal by night[105] and watched at dawn by prince, governor and troops (cf. Dan. 6:19, 24). The innocent man survived and was rescued while the guilty party appears to have got back into the water. The search for him took all morning by the guards who rightly feared what king Nebuchadrezzar would say ('How can we answer the king?'). The king himself then ordered a search by the bridge and every river crossing until the bloated corpse was eventually recovered. This duly attested the folly of doing wrong.

A third (broken) instance related the case of a man who, after

---

[105] A.I. Liederman, *Studies in the Trial by river ordeal in the Ancient Near East* (1974); *RA* 66 (1972), 39–59; 67 (1973), 75–7 (Elam).

charging another took the oath by the god Shamash but refused to stand within the ritual magic circle to do so. Lambert, in publishing this text, has shown that Nebuchadrezzar was but following in the earlier Babylonian tradition of presenting himself in this way as 'the just king' (šar mēšarim). He also considers Nebuchadrezzar to be a Hammurapi *redivivus*, but this impression may be enhanced by the absence of similar records in intervening reigns. Few Babylonian kings attained the reputation of justice to which they aspired, just as kings of Israel and Judah were seldom noted by the Deuteronomist historian for 'doing the right in the eyes of Yahweh.'[106] Lambert may well be justified in seeing this account of Nebuchadrezzar as 'king of Justice' as 'a unique document giving a glimpse of the spiritual revival which accompanied the final burst of Babylonian glory before it sank in the sea of Hellenism.'[107] The text concerning Nebuchadrezzar as šar mēšarim also refers to his royal judgements being written down (ii.25). The surviving fragments of some sixteen legal decisions written in Neo-Babylonian script, orthography and wording and with 'Babylon' in the colophon, may be supporting evidence for this.[108] The recopying of the laws of Hammurapi (c 1750 B.C.) had never ceased for there are Old, and Middle Babylonians and neo-Assyrian texts of them extant. Further copying also took place in Babylon in or soon after the reign of Nebuchadrezzar.[109]

This view of the Babylonian king seemingly concerned with the spiritual and moral issues of life, anxious for divine guidance and working for the spiritual and material welfare of all peoples is no mere propaganda. As a contemporary record it accords with the statements in Daniel where Nebuchadrezzar is shown as willing to accept the interpretation of dreams even when these were later attributed to revelation by a god other than a recognised Babylonian deity to whom he attributed the title 'the most High God' (Dan 2:47; 3:28–29).[110] As Nebuchadrezzar was angry at a miscarriage of justice,[111] so he was roused to fury

---

[106] Wiseman 1973, 17–18.
[107] Lambert 1965, 4.
[108] Driver 1955, 324–7 (against Peiser's dating to Ashurbanipal); ANET 1950, 197.
[109] Wiseman 1962, 161.
[110] This title for Yahweh is used elsewhere by non-Jews (Gen. 14: 18–22; Num. 24:16; Isa. 14:14).
[111] Lambert 1965, 6 (r.iv 11).

at the breaking of a decree (Dan. 3:13).

A further indication of his character is given in a fragmentary epical-historical text published by Grayson[112] which reads:

'Nebuchadrezzar pondered . . . his life was of no value to him . . .[113] he was angry (or stood) and a favourable path (he took . . . and) Babylonia (. . .). To Amēl-Marduk he speaks what was not . . . he then gives a different order but . . . he does not heed the mention of his name (or pronouncement), a courtier. . . . He changed but did not make any obstacle, before . . . . Concerning the fortunes of Esagil and Babylon and . . . the cult-centres of the great gods they considered. . . . He does not have in mind (any concern) for son or daughter, for him there is no family and clan does not exist. . . . In his heart for everything that was abunda(nt. . . .)[114] His attention . . .[115] to promoting the welfare of Esagil (and Babylon). With ears pricked up (eagerly?)[116] he went in through the Holy Gate . . . he prays to the lord of lords, his hands raised (in supplication). He weeps bitterly to his god,[117] the great gods. . . . His prayers go forth to. . . .'

Grayson interprets this as mainly concerned with the unpopular reign of Amēl-Marduk, Nebuchadrezzar's heir, who was later remembered as governing 'public affairs in an arbitary and licentious manner.'[118] The text may indeed refer to a handing over of control temporarily to Amēl-Marduk but if so this is not clear. Jewish legend tells how when Nebuchadrezzar spent seven years among the beasts, high state officials took Amēl-Marduk to make him king in his father's place. A later version, incorporated in Jerome's commentary on Isaiah 14:19, however, says that they refused to do so for fear of Nebuchadrezzar's reappearance.[119] There is no evidence that Amēl-Marduk had a son or daughter or repented for any misdeeds before he was assassinated after a brief reign of two

---

[112] Grayson 1975A, 87–91.

[113] *napištuš la iqēr maharšu*; cf. the attitude of Metati of Zikirtu who then abandoned his capital city (Thureau-Dangin 1912, 18 l. 84).

[114] *duššū*; or possibly *duššu[pat]*, 'sweet'.

[115] *uznūššu* '(in) his ears'.

[116] *turuṣa uznāti* (geštu.11)-šu (l. 15) is used only of animals (AHwB 1448a).

[117] *ilišu* (so Grayson 1975A, 91); cf. Nabopolassar Epic iii 18; Adad-suma-uṣur Epic iii 27 where the name of a specific deity is not needed in confession.

[118] Josephus, *Contra Apionem* I. 12–21; Eusebius, *Chronicorum* I.xi.

[119] Sack 1972, 26 for reference.

years following his father's death. He certainly undertook the
customary support of the temple services and a few repairs.[120]
On the other hand Nebuchadrezzar was renowned for his care of
Esagil and Babylon and according to both Babylonian and
Daniel tradition, was prone to change his mind and orders when
given good grounds to do so.[121] His restoration after banishment
was made with due contrition and acknowledgement that 'The
Most High God is sovereign in the affairs of men' though
Yahweh is not expressly named (Dan. 4:25, 32, 34).

Against this interpretation that the whole of this text, and not
just the first five lines, refers to Nebuchadrezzar, it may be
argued that in the book of Daniel there is confusion, or
substitution, of the name Nabonidus by that of Nebuchadrezzar
to involve the latter more directly in the anti-Jewish debates.
Daniel says 'Nebuchadnezzar . . . was driven away from people,
(lived with the wild animals) and ate grass like cattle. His body
was drenched with the dew of heaven, until his hair grew like the
feathers of an eagle and his nails like the claws of a bird.' (Dan.
4:25, 32–34). He had been told that 'seven times will pass by
until you acknowledge that the Most High is sovereign over the
kingdoms of men and gives them to anyone he wishes.' (v. 25).

The so-called 'Prayer of Nabonidus' (Aramaic text from
Qumran (4QOr Nab) – but some think part of a royal proclamation, (copy of the 1st century A.D.) – reads:

'The words of the [pra]yer said by Nabonidus (nbny), the
king of [the land of Bab]ylon, the [great] king, [when he was
smitten] with malignant boils (šᵉḥinâ) by the ordinance of [God
Most Hig]h in [the city of] Teman: [with malignant boils] I was
smitten for seven years, and so I came to be li[ke the animals;
but I prayed to God Most High] and he pardoned my sins. He
had a diviner, who was a Jewish [man from the exiles, and who
said to me]: 'Make a written proclamation that honour,
[greatness and glory] be given to the name of Go[d Most High.
And so I wrote: when] I was smitten with ma[lignant] boils
[. . .]. In Teman [by the ordinance of God Most High] for
seven years, [I] prayed [and gave praise to] the gods of silver
and gold, [bronze, iron] wood, stone and clay, since [. . .] that
th[ey] were gods [. . .].[Ap]art from these I dreamt [. . .] my

[120] Unger 1928, 361.
[121] Dan. 2:13; 3:19, 30, 46–9; 4:16.

intestines. I could not [. . . .] How much you are like [. . .].'[122]

The similarities between this version and Daniel 4 appear at first to be obvious[123] though the degree of interdependence allowed hangs upon views of the dating of the latter. There are, however, significant differences in the rendering of the royal names, the description of the affliction, the location of the sufferer and the evidence for any literary dependence is not well established.[124] The view that Nabonidus suffered madness is based on a mistranslation of a broken phrase in the Persian Verse account of Cyprus[125] and is compounded by those who took Oppenheim's rendering ('the king is mad' i.e. 'enraged')[126] as indicating insanity![127] Moreover, Nabonidus is known to have been in his self-imposed exile in Teima for ten, not seven, years. Belshazzar was co-regent during his absence and there is no reason to think that Nabonidus 'was driven from the throne' before his ultimate return to Babylon c. 548 and his deportation to Carmania by Cyrus after Belshazzar's death in 539 BC.[128] The motive for Nabonidus' return to Babylonia appears to have been political and due to popular demand following the removal of the threat of fever and famine there.[129]

Nebuchadrezzar's Illness

The description of Nebuchadrezzar's illness in Daniel 4 has led to very diverse interpretations on the assumption that the details given are descriptive and not poetic imagery. The Daniel text implies that the king was put into isolation and slept rough for long enough for his nails to grow like claws. His diet was vegetation ('išba').[130] Insufficient detail of his affliction is given to enable a reliable medical diagnosis to be made such as, for example, that he suffered a psychosomatic form of monomania

---

[122] Jongeling 1976, 123–31; cf. Brownlee 1964, 37.
[123] RB 63 (1956), 405–11; BASOR 145 (1957), 31–82.
[124] Hartman 1962, 81–2.
[125] Smith 1924, 87 i. 17 'an evil demon altered him' render 'his protective deity turned hostile (i.e. unintelligible) to him'.
[126] A.L. Oppenheim, ANET (1950), 314 translates iv. 5 agug šarri 'the king is mad'.
[127] So RB 63 (1966), 410 n.5.
[128] Grayson 1975B, 25, 32 (ii. 21); Josephus, Contra Apionem I 20–1; Eusebius, Evangelium ix. 41.
[129] Gadd 1958, 58; 36–45 cf., 20–2.
[130] Dan. 4:25, cf. vv. 22, 29, 30 (Heb); 5:11 cf. Gen. 1:11 deše' 'eseb; 29 for human consumption.

in which he imagined himself to be an animal (boanthropy).[131] A psychosis analogous to early lycanthropy, from which developed the Middle Ages' legend of the werewolf, has been the customary explanation. Preuss considered it a case of paranoia, since a melancholic would have died of hunger.[132] Lacking other evidence it must suffice to note that the hair and nails left uncut were a sign of mourning.[133] Ahiqar after long concealment was said to have appeared with fingernails like the talons of a bird and with overgrown hair.[134] As a former official of the court of Sennacherib and Esarhaddon in the seventh century, stories about Ahiqar were remembered into the Seleucid and later periods, as were those about Nebuchadrezzar and Daniel. A Babylonian text copied in Uruk on 14th July 165 B.C. gives the Babylonian name of Ahiqar as 'Aba-^{d}Enlil-dari: whom the Aramaeans (Ahlamû) call Ahu'qāri: (In Greek) he is Niqaquru'.[135]

This episode in Nebuchadrezzar's life, which the recovery of any Babylonian Chronicle for the relevant years alone might solve, raises the question of the state of medical knowledge at the time. Essential medical reference books used by the Babylonian 'physician' (asû) and 'exorcist/magician/psychologist' (āšipu) were known and copied. These include tablets 1–31 of the diagnostic series 'when an āšipu enters the house of a sick man' (šumma ana bīt marṣi).[136] The tradition of making copies of this text in Babylonia, mainly in Babylon and Borsippa, runs from Marduk-apla-iddina II (c. 710) at least to the latest known from the eleventh year of Artaxerxes I (453 B.C.).[137] Other medical texts surviving through this same period and on to the time of Alexander include the Vade mecum, therapy texts relating to the head and to specific diseases, and a treatise on poultices (mêlu),[138] lists of illnesses, prescriptions for nasal ailments, commentaries on medical texts, medical recipes and others.[139] A tablet bearing an inscription for the treatment of skin diseases

---

[131] ISBF I (1976), 956.
[132] Rosner 1978, 311.
[133] Deut. 21:12; Mo'ed Kaṭan 18a.
[134] E. Yamauchi, Greece and Babylon (1967), 87.
[135] UVB 18 (1962), 45, 51–2 (ll. 20–1).
[136] E.g. Labat 1951, p. xiv; Tablets 2, 12; BM. 33424, 38362, 38530, 47753 (Tablet 25), 50242 (Tablet 28 from Sippar), all unpublished; Hunger 1976, No. 27.
[137] Labat 1951, Tablet 2B (BM. 76522, 35).
[138] Köcher 1963, Nos. 478, 479, 481, 536–7.

was found carefully laid in a grave of the sixth-fifth century, though there is otherwise no known tradition in Mesopotamia for putting inscriptions of any kind with a corpse.[140]

At the least these texts indicate the state of medical knowledge available to help Nebuchadrezzar at his court. They contradict Oppenheim's supposition that medicine had at this time dropped out of the curriculum in Babylonia and was possibly practised by those whose training was based solely on experience and oral training.[141] This view may have been influenced by the later statement of Herodotus on what he considered one of the wisest of Babylonian institutions: 'They have no physicians, but when a man is ill they lay him in the square (*agora*), and the passers-by come up to him, and if they have ever had this disease themselves or have known anyone who has suffered from it, they give him advice, recommending him to do whatever they found good in their case, or in the case known to them. No one is allowed to pass the sick man in silence without asking him what his ailment is.'(I.197) There is no evidence that the Babylonians were treated in public,[142] while there is some to show that a sick room was associated with a temple, though perhaps for its servants, for there is a case of a midnight call for medical advice by superiors to come to the area set aside for female patients.[143] Herodotus seems to have confused Babylonian and Assyrian customs in telling of a woman having to offer herself publicly for some form of temple prostitution on behalf of Aphrodite 'the goddess called Mylitta by the Assyrians' (I.199). Release was only after submission to any stranger who threw her a silver coin to follow him. At Assur lead discs with pornographic scenes on them were discovered in the precincts of the temple of Ishtar.[144] These may have been connected with some similar custom in Babylon since Mylitta may be a rendering of Mulissu, the Neo-Assyrian form of the Akkadian name of the goddess Ninlil (Old Babylonian *Mulliltum*). The same divine element is found in the personal name Arda-Mulišši which Parpola identifies with

---

[139] Hunger 1976, Nos. 43, 45, 48–55, 59–68, (44, 46, 47).
[140] Biggs 1969, 101.
[141] Oppenheim 1962, 104.
[142] *JEA* 10 (1924), 179.
[143] *MAOG* X/I (1926), 26 ff. (*c.* 1350 B.C.); cf. *JRAS* 1926, 689.
[144] CAH I.2 (1971) 259.

Adrammelech, one of the murderers of Sennacherib (2 Kings 19:37) named by Berossus Adramelos (Ardumuzan).[145]

Babylon: City of Refuge

Babylon may have served also as a special place of sanctuary, for one of its titles in the Topography was 'the privileged place for the freeing of the bound,' (i.e. the release of prisoners; uru.šar.ṣi.il.du.a.(ki): *āl kidinnu pāṭiri kasî*).[146] This expression could be taken as an allusion to Babylon as a place of high medical repute where sicknesses were cured, for *kasû paṭāru* is elsewhere commonly associated with this.[147] On the other hand Babylon in the preceeding half-century is referred to in a letter by another of its titles, 'the bond of the lands' (*rikis mātāti*), to which 'if, anyone enters his protection (*kidinnu*) is assured' (ABL 878). The same letter mentions a building in Babylon designated for the granting of freedom (*purur*) and continues 'no dog who has entered is put to death (*iddak*)'. This may well refer to those citizens, even as evil doers, who were granted *kidinnu* rights. In *The Tale of the Poor Man of Nippur*, another temple-city granted similar privileges, the Mayor calls upon his attacker Gimil-Ninurta 'not to destroy a citizen of Nippur and not to stain your hand with the blood of a *kidinnu*-protected person sacred to Enlil'.[148] Also a man claiming that he had been unjustly imprisoned, probably within Babylon, writes that on release he offered a prayer that the king would come and re-establish the *kidinnūtu* of Babylon.[149] There appears then to be a sense in which the city was considered a place of freedom from oppression. Thus the royal protection (*ṣulūlu*) granted to one of *kidinnu*-status is explained by the equation of 'men of *kidinnu*' with 'those liberated (*šubarē*) by the great gods.'[150] While this may be descriptive of nothing more than the exemptions (*zakūtu*) and freedom from taxation and service (*andurāru*) conferred by it, it cannot merely denote the granting

---

[145] Alster 1980, 174, 177 n.21;
[146] Gurney 1974, 57 (l. 10).
[147] STT I 72, 100; *AMT* 71 1:34; *KAR* 228, 4; 321:1.
[148] STT I 106; *An.St.* 6 (1956), 154–5; cf. *JCS* 27 (1975), 163–74; 31 (1979), 189–215.
[149] ABL 1431:4.
[150] VAS I. 39 iii, 10ff.; Borger 1956, 25 (Ep. 37); cf. 21 (Ep. 23:18), 26 (Ep. 38:34); UET I (1928), 50 187:7.

of asylum to refugees (*maqtu*) or refer to Babylon as the noted cult-centre to which deities from nearby cities were brought in for safety in time of war. Such harbouring was expected by the neighbouring population as a right. Nebuchadrezzar would surely have confirmed this privileged position of his city, as had his predecessar Marduk-apla-iddina II, as part of his policy of uniting the surrounding tribes.[151] The status was fresh in the minds of the older citizens, having been reaffirmed by Ashurbanipal and Šamaš-šum-ukīn[152] and again in the New Year Festival ritual in which Nebuchadrezzar and his father participated.[153]

The rôle of the temple as sanctuary was well known in Syria-Palestine throughout the first millennium.[154] It was to avoid offending the populace unnecessarily by breaching local customs and taboos that invaders of Babylon who respected its religious and cultural heritage gave orders to their troops not to enter certain privileged centres. A text from Babylon (BM. 36761) dated 330/29 B.C. provides a glimpse of what appears to be local report on Alexander's entry into Babylon when the same precautions were taken (see Appendix 1, Fig. 14).[155] Some of these places were distinguished by the *kidinnu*-symbol over the gate. The prohibition may also have been associated with that against carrying weapons there. It was said of rebels that 'they even drew the sword in Nineveh which is a godless thing to do.'[156] Oppenheim has compared this with European *Burgfriede*.[157] The same prohibition may explain the view of *kidinnu* as *Marktfriede*,[158] though the latter could have been due to the obvious advantages to be gained in Babylon as a commercial centre by allowing certain privileges to be extended to those who entered the city for the purposes of transport and trade.

---

[151] See also p. 79; Reviv 1985, 6–7; Brinkman 1964.

[152] ABL 926, 11.

[153] Thureau-Dangin 1921, 130 ll. 31–2; 135, l. 264.

[154] I Sam. 19:18 (Ramah); 1 Kings 1:50–1; 2:28; 19:3 (Beersheba); Neh. 6:10; 1 Macc. 16:43 cf. Aharoni 1981, 37 (No. 18 'he is in the House of Yahweh'); *Supp. Dict. Bible* (1979), 1480–1510 espec. 1483–1485.

[155] So Alexander the Great on entry to Babylon (BM. 36761 published in Appendix, p.121).

[156] Borger 1956, 42:23.

[157] Oppenheim 1964, 121.

[158] Leemans 1946, 36f.; Reviv. 1985, n.41.

Other Traditions

Most commentators today view episodes incorporated into the historical introduction to the Book of Daniel (1–6) as late midrash. Attention is particularly drawn to the dedication of the golden statue and the punishments meted out to the Jewish defaulters by burning in a very hot furnace or by being cast into a den of fierce lions, from both of which they were delivered miraculously by divine intervention. Some observations may be relevant to the debate in the light of evidence from Neo-Babylonian times.

The huge statue set up to be worshipped in the Dura plain (Dan. 3:1–12) has given rise to much speculation. The statue is presumed to be that of a deity though nowhere is this expressly stated, but probably indicated, by the call 'to fall down and worship the image' and 'serve your gods' (Dan. 3:10–12, 18). If the image was not of the king claiming obeisence as 'king of kings' (Dan. 2:37–38) then it would be expected to represent the city-god Marduk. Dossin has suggested that even the name Marduk was by learned and complicated sophistry equated with the name of the city *Bāb-ili* through the use of rare syllabic equivalents of the logograms used. The complexity of reading dingir = mar = (eme.sal) gar = *ilu* and ká = ka = *dug/k* giving *duk* + *mar* inverted to read Marduk is of a type not otherwise unattested but confined to the limited circles of a few Babylonian schools.[159] Such reasoning would not be necessary to the ancient Babylonian bowing before the principal god of his city and land.

The suggestion that the obeisence of the whole population of Babylon was part of a religious reformation introduced by Nebuchadrezzar involving congregational worship, as a substitute for the more intimate ritual normally performed by priests, finds little support. Woolley considered his discovery of a remodelled building and raised outer court of the Nannar temple at Ur, as reconstructed by Nebuchadrezzar, to be an example of this. However, this interpretation of his finds there is no longer followed[160] and no significant changes in the ori-

---

[159] Dossin 1981, 1–2.
[160] UE 5 (1962), 24.

entation or layout of any indisputably religious building of his reign has yet been traced.[161]

The statue could have been that of the king to which all officials and vassals had to swear on loyalty oath, perhaps in his absence. Calmeyer has shown that one function of the images of kings placed outside a gateway and by a wall (*dūru*) in Achaemenid times was to provide a permanent symbol of his ownership of the palace, city or territory and also served to represent him in his absence.[162] It could have marked the symbolic presence of the king as judge on his throne by the city-gate, as that of Shalmaneser III at Assur,[163] or the portrait of the same king in a glazed-brick panel found near an entrance to Fort Shalmaneser, Kalhu.[164] The relief of the king performing political and religious function was common in such positions and could well have served in some way to denote his continued authority even though not present. Though such representations are not directly attested in Achaemenid times Philostratos in his *Life of Apollonius* (I.27), written in the late second century A.D. to describe Parthian Mesopotamia but sometimes including older material, states:

'When then he (Apollonius of Tyana) arrived at Babylon, the satrap in command of the great gates having learned that he had come to see the country, held out a golden image of the king, towards which everyone must make *proskynesis* before he is allowed to enter the city. Now an ambassador coming from the Roman Emperor has not this ceremony imposed upon him, but anyone who comes from the barbarians or just to look at the country, is arrested with dishonour unless he has first paid his respect to this image.' Some such ceremony may also lie behind the incident of the outstretched sceptre in Esther 5:2.[165]

The place of erection of the statue is given as 'the plain of Dura in the (judicial) district of Babylon' (Dan. 3:1, *baqᵉᶜaṯ dûrā' bimᵉdînaṯ bābel*).[166] The location of Dura (Aram. Dûra',

[161] cf. Fig. 9 (Nabû temple lay-out).

[162] P. Calmeyer, 'Textual Sources for the Interpretation of Achaemenid Palace Decorations', *Iran* 18 (1980) 55–63.

[163] BM. 849; A.H. Layard, *Inscriptions in the cuneiform character from Assyrian Monuments* (1851), pl. 76f.; L. Messerschmidt, *Keilschrifttexte aus Assur: Historischen Inhalts* (1911) I Nr. 30.

[164] *Iraq* 25 (1963) 38 and possibly at Kalhu (*Iraq* 21 (1960) 147.

[165] Some such ceremony may lie behind the incident in Esther 5:2.

[166] *bq'* perhaps, 'breech' or 'opening'.

LXX Δεειρα) has given rise to speculation. Since it was near Babylon it could have been by the (fortified) city-wall (*dūru*)[167] parts of which were specifically named (e.g. *Dūru ša karābi*).[168] Oppert identified it with Dura south-south-east of Babylon where brick structures were found.[169] Tell Dēr *c.* 50 km north of Babylon is a possibility but attempts to site Dura further afield are against the context. Borger proposed an equation with Tell al Lahm near Ur[170] but against this Michalowski considered it to be the same as the Ur III Dēr, a military centre near Uruk.[171]

The image at 60 cubits high would be a third lower than the top of the Etemenanki upper shrine. The dimensions of 27 × 2.7 m. have been questioned and it may be asked if the Aram. *šittîn* (sixty) could here (and Ezra 6:3) stand for another unit of dimension.[172] Alternatively the smaller statue could have been set on a plinth at a high level. The use of a herald for public proclamations was a long-standing Babylonian tradition.[173] The mention of the orchestra would be another indication that the event was a court affair, perhaps the dedication of the statue. Foreign musicians were known to be at Nebuchadrezzar's court, as they were at others.[174] This could account for the names of some of the instruments given in Aramaic as the 'horn' (*qarā*, 'pipe' or 'flute' (*masrôqîta*), 'lyre' or 'zither' (*qayt̲ᵉrās*), 'trigon' or 'lyre' (*sabbᵉkā*, 'triangular harp' (*pᵉsantērîn*), '(bag) pipes' (*sûmponᵉyâ*) 'and all kinds of music (melody and/or singing)?' (Dan. 3:5, 10). The studies by Mitchell and Joyce and by Coxon have shown that all these types of instruments, perhaps better translated as 'horn, flute, zither, lyre and pipes in unison', occur in early Babylonian and early Greek texts. Thus *symphōnia* can be compared with the adjective *symphōnous* in *Hymni Homerici ad Mercurium 51*. The *kithera* was also known in Homeric times (*kitharis*, *Iliad* 13, 731; *Odyssey* I:153), but the *sambukē*, a foreign word in Greek, could have entered

---

[167] *dūr bābili*, *An.Or* 60 r.12 (time of Cyrus).
[168] Langdon 1912, 74 ii. 22.
[169] *Expéd. Scientifique en Mésopotamie* I (1862), 238–40.
[170] *ZA* 65 (1975), 219f.
[171] *Mesopotamia* 12 (1977), 83–96 (possibly Umm al-Wawīya).
[172] Cf. Akkad. *šittān* 'two kinds'. If this were interpreted as 'twenty' cubits, as some suggest, it would imply that 'Darius the Mede' of Dan. 5:31 (Heb. 6:1) was 'twenty-two' which is unlikely (Wiseman 1965, 14–15). Berger 1975, 223 compares the size of the statue with the Colossus of Rhodes constructed more than a hundred years earlier.
[173] *Sumer* 20 (1964), 66:3; Atrahasīs 68 I, 376; Lambert 1960, 112:25; VAS I 37 v.7.
[174] Kinnier Wilson 1972, 76–8.

Greece early and be better known in its Aramaic speaking homeland. Traditional as well as foreign, and innovational, music was common at the courts of kings whose sway covered widespread territories.[175]

The punishment of Daniel's companions for failing to bow to the image was to be placed in a furnace 'heated seven times hotter than usual' (Daniel 3:19). Massive furnaces must have been used to fire the estimated fifteen million kiln-fired, as well as glazed, bricks required for Nebuchadrezzar's numerous building operations.[176] These were usually fired to about 850–950 centigrade but a higher temperature could be obtained by the use of wood fires or the equally available bitumen from Hit. The tradition of the later committal of Daniel's companions to a den of lions is not an improbable one in that lions from cages were hunted, as a trial of royal prowess, in the *ambassu* or royal parklands from the days of Tilgathpileser I onwards.[177] The lion at Babylon was a major symbol of the god Marduk and so frequently of 'the dog of Ishtar' depicted on the Ishtar Gate and the Hittite representation of the conqueror[178] kept in Nebuchadrezzar's 'Museum' and similarly represented on palace furniture elsewhere.[179] In his training days Daniel might well have copied the line in the Babylonian story of the righteous sufferer (*ludul bēl nēmeqi*) which read 'It was Marduk who put a muzzle on the mouth of the lion who was eating me', or the delivered man's word that it was 'Marduk deprived my pursuer of his sling and turned aside his slingstones.'[180]

Nebuchadrezzar's Death and Burial

It is surprising that, if as some suppose, the later Old Testament documents stem from the Maccabean or Hellenistic

[175] Wiseman 1965, 19–27; P. W. Coxon, *Glasgow University Oriental Society Transactions* 25 (1973/4 pub. 1976); 24–40.

[176] Koldewey 1914, 82; such bricks are found in Nebuchadrezzar's quay wall as far north as Baghdad itself. On the 'fiercely blazing furnace of Dan. 3:11, 19 cf. *Tyndale Bulletin*

[177] Barnett 1976, espec. pls. V, IX, XIII, XV; Streck 1916, 308d ('For my pleasure they let a fierce lion of the desert out of his cage'). The lion-cage is *nabārti ša nēšē* (Hg.A.I.95f.).

[178] *Or.* 34 (1965), 108:6 (namburbi).

[179] Koldewey 1914, 160–1 (fig. 101); M.E.L. Mallowan, *Nimrud and its Remains* I (1966), 139.

[180] Lambert 1960, 56 (Ludlul bēl Nēmeqi Commentary q,r).

periods, there is no triumphant reference to the death of Nebuchadrezzar, as of Belshazzar (Dan 5:30), in vindication of God's deliverance of his exiled people. But this is implied in subsequent narratives as it is, failing the survival of the Babylonian Chronicle for the year, in the Babylonian texts. Nebuchadrezzar's son Amēl-Marduk succeeded him in 562 (cf. Jer. 52:31). Since the last tablet dated by his regnal years is 8 October 562 at Uruk[181] and the first dated to his successor Amēl-Marduk as King of Babylon on the same day,[182] it is assumed that Nebuchadrezzar died during the first days of October 562 B.C.[183] This has been questioned by Weisberg since he interprets a text about the hire of a woman *šerku*, dated at an otherwise unknown place on 29 August 562 as a new form of dating by 'The goddess of Uruk, king of Babylon' indicating that Nebuchadrezzar may have died earlier and that a cautious scribe continued to date by him 'even after his death, waiting prudently to see who his successor would be.'[184] Against this, no other dating by a deity is known elsewhere in first millennium texts and the practice of an interregnum was marked by either continuing to name the previous ruler or by indicating the date by a post(*arki*)-regnal formula.[185] The evidence is therefore doubtful since in other cities Nebuchadrezzar's later rule is attested by the dates given. However, it should be also noted that Sack considered the possibility that Nebuchadrezzar died earlier than October on the basis of two contracts from Sippar dated to earlier months by Amēl-Marduk's accession year, 4 August and 4 (−12?) September 562. While thinking this unlikely he used the evidence of these texts as the basis of a proposed coregency between Nebuchadrezzar and his son.[186] However, such a co-regency would not be reflected in a year formula until the Seleucid period or later[187] though a co-regency

[181] TCL XII, 58; cf. unpublished text NCBT 286 (*JNES* 3 (1944), 44).

[182] B.T.A. Evetts, *Inscriptions of the Reigns of Evil-Merodach, Neriglissar and Laborosarchod* (1892), No. 1 (Sippar, 26. VI. Acc. Amēl-Marduk).

[183] Parker and Dubberstein 1956, 12. The latest known dating by Nebuchadrezzar at Babylon is 12. VI. 43 year (25 Sept. 562 B.C. in BM. 37328 (unpublished).

[184] Weisberg 1980, xix, 9, 16 (No. 9:16).

[185] Wiseman 1981, 568.

[186] Sack 1972, 3, 90 (No. 56: BM. 80920 r.4'), 106 (No. 79; BM. 58872:12).

[187] E.G. Antiochus and Seleucus on dating formulae (e.g. BM. 33816, 41159). Wiseman, *BSOAS* 37 (1974), 451 (citing BM. 34787 unpublished) refers to texts giving alternative names for the same person, 'accession year of Ochus who is called Darius'.

arrangement for a king who had reigned forty-three years is probable.[188] The collated reading of one of the two texts cited leaves the matter open to doubt and it would be wiser to await confirmation of such an arrangement from another source.[189] This is all the more so since a scribe at Babylon itself continued to date documents by Nebuchadrezzar's regnal years as late as 24 September 562.[190]

The Babylonian Chronicle, were it extant, might well have given the precise date of Nebuchadrezzar's death as it had for his father.[191] His burial would have been hardly less elaborate than that accorded to the aged Queen-Mother Adad-Guppi' by Nabonidus in 547 B.C. He prepared her corpse for burial (šalmassu ukammis), clothing it in a splendid coloured and bejewelled robe and anointing it with sweet oil before it was placed in a secluded or hidden place (iškuna ina niṣirti).[192] The internment was then attended by the people of Babylon and Borsippa as well as by representatives from the entire empire from the border of Egypt to the Persian Gulf including kings, princes and governors. After seven days and nights of mourning all were feasted before returning home.[193] There is no sure clue to the location of the royal necropolis at or near Babylon unless it was associated with the mortuary temple, mausoleum or 'House of the Dead' (é.nam.úš,bīt mūti) mentioned in the Topography as in the Kumar quarter.[194] If it lay in the West Wall near a gate it could have given rise to the strange legend of the tomb of Nitocris recounted by Herodotus (I.187).[195] The brick-built subterranean chambers with barrel shaped vaulting, similar to those in the necropolis at Assur, found in the Merkes, could be tombs of nobles or part of a reused drainage system. Since bronze coffins are attested in the late eighth-seventh B.C. at Ur analagous with terracotta examples found at Babylon for the

---

[188] Wiseman, loc. cit., 452.

[189] Sack 1972, No. 70: 3 dated at Uruk (?) 29. IV. access. Amēl-Marduk (cf. Wiseman, BSOAS 37 (1974), 451).

[190] BM. 37328 (12.VI.43 Neb; unpublished).

[191] Wiseman 1956, 68; Grayson 1975, 99.

[192] niṣirtu as a description of the tomb (E. Ebeling, Tod und Leben nach den Vorstellungen der Babylonier, Berlin 1931, 57:7).

[193] Gadd 1958, 50 iii 10–44.

[194] 1.27; cf. é.kur.bad=é mu-ti (CT 18 30 r.i.29; Luckenbill 1924, 151 XIII.1 (é.gal tapšuhti); XIV.2 (kimāh tapšuhti) for Sennacherib's royal sepulchre at Ashur. A family tomb was kimāh kimtišu.

[195] I. 187; Unger 1931, 161 and Herodotus I. 198 for Babylonian funerary customs.

PLATE I

a. Gardens shown on Assyrian sculpture at Nineveh c. 640 B.C. (BM. 124939)

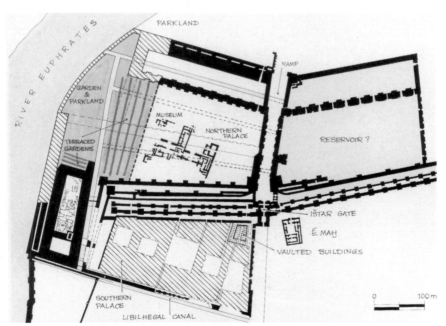

b. Proposed location of the Royal ('Hanging') Gardens at Babylon

PLATE II

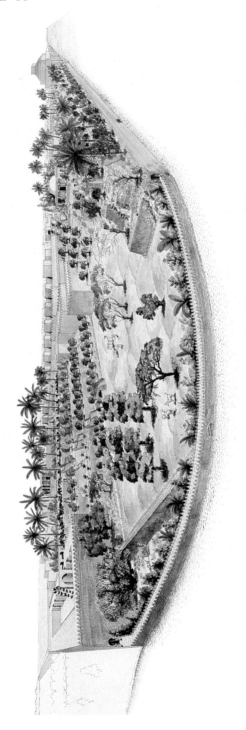

Reconstruction of the Royal Gardens at Babylon

PLATE III

a. The Nabû ša harē temple, viewed from east

b. View inside temple to south showing offering tables

PLATE IV

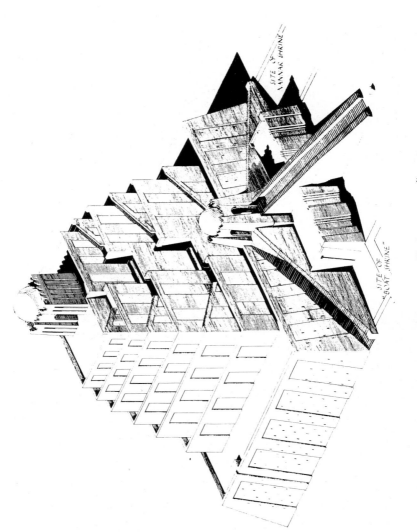

SITE OF KANNAR SHRINE

SITE OF "BOAT SHRINE"

Ziggurat of Nabonidus at Ur (reconstructed)

PLATE V

Ah'ūtu text showing plan of the ideal ziggurat (see also Fig. 12 p. 72)

PLATE VI

The Babylonian Chronicle (BM.21946) recording the Battle of Carchemish in 605 B.C. (obverse, above) and the Capture of Jerusalem in 597 B.C. (reverse, below)

PLATE VII

a. The southern citadel

b. The Ishtar Gateway

Babylon. Excavation and restoration, 1979

PLATE VIII

a. The Temple of Ishtar

b. Stamped Brick Inscription of Nebuchadrezzar II

same period it is possible that one could have been used for the internment of King Nebuchadrezzar.[196] Mār-Ištar, responsible for keeping the Assyrian court informed of affairs in Babylonia, had earlier written of the preparation of a tomb or mausoleum (é.ki.mah) in Babylon for an Assyrian 'substitute king' (šar puhi). This person was presumably a native Babylonian.[197] The practice of bringing a person of distinction home for burial is attested.[198] It is possible that Nebuchadrezzar was buried in his home tribal area at or near Uruk, but a burial place for the new dynasty near the citadel of Babylon and overlooking the river would be expected by compromise with that practised at Assur. The later tradition that Amēl-Marduk removed his father's corpse from the grave and disposed of it is usually attributed to late Jewish fable which ascribes this to the instigation of Jehoiachin as part of the Jewish vengeance on their hated conqueror.[199]

These Lectures have sought to portray some of the background, historical, physical and intellectual, of the early period of the Jewish exile in Babylonia. It requires no profound theological appraisal to realise that many devout Jews would have reacted against the alien philosophy pervading the culture that surrounded them there. Amid the splendour of the great walled city which they may have helped to rebuild they longed for the reinstatement and revival of Jerusalem as their own national capital. Amid the glamour of the worship of the many bejewelled deities their thoughts would have turned to the One God — for them unrepresentable even as he was then unrepresented in any temple there or back home. Amid the clamour of the multi-racial metropolis the exiles must have watched the kings of many nations bring their tribute to Nebuchadrezzar and have envisaged the long-promised Day when the same would be done not for a man but for their God as King of Kings in his new city.

---

[196] Koldewey 1914, 275 (for brick vaults); E. Stromenger, 'Grabformen in Babylon' in *Baghdader Mitteilungen* 3 (1964), 157–73; J Curtis, 'Late Assyrian Bronze Coffins' in *An. St.* 33 (1983), 85–95

[197] ABL 437; cf. ABL 1215 ('weeping in Esagila').

[198] Brinkman 1968 155, n.934, 'in a place befitting a legitimate king'; cf. ibid. 143, 6 for the burial of Ea-mukīn-zēri a usurper in the awamp of Bīt-Hašmar. For the transport of corpses see Streck 1916, 60 vii.40. Salt may have been used as a preservative on long journeys (CAD 11.1, 206 sub. *nâlu*)

[199] Sack 1972, 26–9: cf. P.R.S. Moorey, 'Where did they bury the Kings of the IIIrd Dynasty of Ur?', in *Iraq* 46 (1984), 16–18 for burials outside the main citadel.

Appendix: *Alexander in Babylon*

Apart from a few statements in Hellenistic sources little has been known of Alexander the Great in Babylonia. He is named (*ʹA-lik-sa-an-dar*) in Babylonian King Lists dating from the Seleucid era, though these are without significant chronological data other than the length of his reign of seven years.[1] A fragmentary Dynastic Prophecy from Babylon (BM. 40623 iii 9–23) follows a brief two line description of the five year reign of Darius (III) with a statement of an attack by the army of the Greeks (*Hanî*) after which a king is said to have refitted his army to take up arms again. This is usually interpreted as the defeat of Darius at Issus. The text then appears to 'prophecy' that the king, with the help of the gods of Babylon, will defeat the Greeks and carry off extensive booty to his palace. 'The people who have experienced misfortune will enjoy well-being. The mood of the land (will be a happy one). Tax exemption. . . .'[2] The proven accuracy of this and similar chronicle-type texts makes it very unlikely that Alexander's victory would be falsified. One possible solution could be that this whole section refers to Alexander's victory at Gaugamela and that it was he who re-equipped his army in Babylon and brought spoil into the city. The Babylonians would have interpreted the gods as 'going at the side of his army' as demonstrated by the victory. However the line at present interpreted as 'the overthrow of the army of the Hanean he will (bring about)' would then need to be taken as 'he will (grant) a rest/respite for the Hanean/Greek army' or the like.[3] The following lines could well mean that Alexander carried off extensive booty from Babylon, much as he did from Persepolis and Susa in the next year. The happy reception by the people and the tax-exemption agrees well with Alexander's reputation there and the designation of his reign as 'good' fits in with the 'prophetical' scheme of the text.[4]

---

[1] A.J. Sachs and D.J. Wiseman, 'A Babylonian King List of the Hellenistic Period', *Iraq* 16 (1954), 203–4; J. van Dijk, *UVB* 18 (1962), 58–60, pl. 28 (=ANET 566).

[2] Grayson 1975A, 26, 34–5.

[3] A *sukuptu (sakāpu* II) is however not attested elsewhere.

[4] Cf. Grayson 1975A, 27, and n.14.

A broken text may refer to these same events and period (BM. 36761 = 80–6–17, 476 see Fig. 14). The astronomical observations cited in ll. 1′–10′ enable it to be dated to months VI/VII 330 B.C.[5] As is customary in such astronomical diaries these are followed by current prices of staple commodities for that month (here of oil and wool) and by the signs of the zodiac in which the five planets were at the time. Finally, notices of any noteworthy happenings as known in Babylon were appended.[6]

These historical observations refer to the eleventh day of an unnamed month[7] when there was panic or fear in the military camp (of the Babylonians?). An army (the Greeks?) lay (encamped) confronting the king. On the twenty-fourth in the morning its king raised the standard (zakiptu) . . .[8] After a break there is reference to a fierce clash in terms reminiscent of the great battle between Nebuchadrezzar's forces and the Egyptians in 601 B.C.[9] Someone abandons his army, his army personnel return to their cities and an individual seems to have disappeared into the land of Guti. Until a join is made with other, as yet unidentified, fragments of this large unpublished class of cuneiform texts, little more can be gleaned from this text at present. The contents are strikingly similar to the events of the epic battle at Gaugamela, near Karamlais between Kirkuk and Erbil. There Alexander's forces bivouaced while the Persians nervously stood at arms all night. Alexander himself led his army out next morning and a mighty battle ensued, the outcome of which was in the balance until Darius, as at Issus, fled into the Persian hills (Gutî) abandoning his army. There were considerable losses on both sides.[10]

The date of the battle is usually given as 1 October, 331 B.C.

[5] LBART p. xiii, No. 196, cf. p. vii. BM. 36761 I identified, with A.J. Sachs, among some thousand astronomical diaries and related astronomical texts in 1951. It was originally planned to publish the fragments containing historical data in a separate volume, but the untimely death of Professor Sachs thwarted this. This isolated text is, however, now published by permission of the Trustees of the British Museum.

[6] See p. 29; Sachs 1948, 286.

[7] L.13′; i.e. 7 September 330 if the reference is to month VI.

[8] Taking zakiptu as an emblem bringing victory as in the Nabopolassar Epic (Grayson 1975A, 84 iii 7) rather than as a mark of coronation or kingship (ibid. l. 10; see p. 20).

[9] Cf. ina tāhāz ṣēri irta ahāmeš imhaṣūma dabdâ [. . .iškunū. . . BM. 21946 r.7; Wiseman 1956, 70.

[10] W.W. Tarn, Alexander the Great (1948) I, 49–51; II, Appendix 5.

This text seems to place it at the end of September 330 B.C., but this does not preclude any equation between this diary and the classical sources since two systems of dating were then in use. The one reckoned Alexander's first year as ruler of Babylonia as beginning in the year commencing 3 April 330 B.C., the other counted from his accession as ruler of Macedon (Bab. *makkadunû*), i.e. year 1 as 336, since the Macedonians did not employ the 'accession year' dating common in Babylonian practice but dropped in Babylonia itself from Alexander onwards.[11]

The reverse of tablet BM. 36761 follows prices with historical notices beginning on the first of an unnamed month, possibly VII beginning 27 September 330, Alexander 1.[12] From the broken text it may be judged that some persons came down to Babylon where the citizens or others did something in relation to the property of the Esagil temple there. Perhaps this was a precautionary measure of taking goods or other items such as statuary into the sanctuary for safekeeping on the approach of the enemy. Then on the eleventh day[13] in Sippar, north of Babylon, Alexander seems to have issued an order that no one should enter their buildings, probably the holy places rather than private dwellings.[14] Two days later the next episode took place at the outer gate of Esagil. After two more days[15] the Greek (^{lú}*iamanāya* is mentioned together with reference to something or some persons reduced in numbers or status and to sacrifices. Alexander (^{I}*alexandaris*) as ruler or king (*šarru*) entered Babylon apparently with horses and the accoutrements of war to be received by 'the citizens of Babylon and the people'. In the lacunae some reference may have been made to the part played in this welcome by Mazaeus. If the identification of this fragment is upheld it provides some confirmation from Babylonian sources of Alexander's conquest of their territory and capital – a matter of renowned historical moment.

---

[11] Parker and Dubberstein 1956, 19 and n.4.
[12] Since most astronomical diaries cover a period of six months this remains a tentative suggestion.
[13] 7 October if month VII.
[14] See p. 108.
[15] Possibly 11 October 330 B.C.

Transliteration (BM. 36761)
Obv.

12'. še.giš 1 pi síg.há 5 ma⁽ˢⁱᶜ⁾ *i-nu-šú* mul.babbar *ina* gír.tab.dele[bat. . . .

13'. itu.bi u₄–11-kám *hat-tu₄ ina ma-dak-tu₄ ina qud-me* lugal *š*[*á*. . .]

14'. *ana tar-ṣi* lugal šub^ú 24-kám *ina še-rim* lugal-*šú za-qip-t*[*u₄*. . . .

15'. gab *a-ha-meš im-ha-ṣu-ma* ši.ši lú.erim.meš *kab-t*[*ù-ti iškunū* . . .

16'. lú.erim.meš-*šú ú-maš-šìr ú-lim-ma ana* uru.meš-*šú-nu* [. . .

17'. [*ina m*]*āt*ˡ *gu-ti-i* záh^ⁱˡ⁻ʾ [. . . .

Translation

12'. 'Oil 1 pi wool 5 shek[els]. At that time Jupiter in Scorpio.

13'. On day 11 of that month there was panic in the military camp. Before the king [. . . .

14'. pitched camp facing the king. On (day) 24 in the morning its king (set up) the standard [. . . .

15'. They fought one another and inflicted a defeat. impor[tant officers . . . .

16'. He abandoned his army . . . to their cities [. . . .

17'. [In the] land of Guti he disappeared/faintness [. . . .

Transliteration

reverse

1'. [. . . .

2'. [še *a*]-*na* 1 gǐn 1 [. . . .

3'. [i]tu.bi ta 1 e[n?. . . .

4'. *ana* e.ki du.*ku-um-ma* é.sag.íl. .[. . . .

5'. *u* dumu.meš e.ki *a-na* nǐg.ga é.sag.íl . . [. . . .

6'. u₄–11-kám *ina* ^ᵘʳᵘzimbir^ki *ṭè-e-mu šá* ˡ*a-*ˡ*lik*ˡ-[*sa-an-dar-ri-is*. . . .

7'. [. .] . . *a-na* é.meš-*ku-nu ul ir-ru-ub* u₄–13-kám [. . . .

8'. [.. .. ..]*te*ʾ ká *ka-mi-i šá* é.sag.gíl *ù k*[*i*?. . . .

9'. [.. .. ..] u₄–15-kám ^ˡúˡ*ia-ma-na-a-a mu-tim* gu₄[. . . .

10'. [.. .. ..] lúgud.da.meš uzu me gan.[. . . .

11'.   [.. .. ..¹]*a-lik-sa-an-dar-ri-is* lugal-*šú ana* e^{ki} [. . . .
12'.   [anše.k]ur.ra.meš (erasure) *ù ú-nₗu-utₗ* [. . .
13.   [. . .] *u* dumu.meš e^{ki} *u* ukù.meš [. . . .
14.   [. . .]*ši-piš-tú šá* lugal[. . . .
15.   [. . .] ra-ma- [. . . .

Translation

1.   '. . .
2.   barley for 1 shekel 1 . . .
3.   In that month from . . .
4.   came to Babylon. Esagil . . .
5.   and the citizens of Babylon to the property of Esagil . . .
6.   On day 11 in Sippar. An order/report that Alexander . . .
7.   . . . shall not go into your buildings. On day 13 . . .
8.   . . . the outer gate of Esagil and . . .
9.   . . . on day 15 the Greek, . . .
10.   . . . those deprived, flesh . . .
11.   . . . Alexander its king to Babylon entered? . . .
12.   (Hor)ses and implements of war . . .
13.   . . . and the citizens of Babylon and the people . . .
14.   . . . a message . . .
15.   . . . .'

Notes

Obv.

13.   *madaktu*; cf. BM. 36304 r.12' (Grayson 1975, 112) a damaged chronicle customarily attributed to Xerxes I. It could however, refer to Darius III (l. 7'); note the parallel phrases *ummān Hanî* (l. 6') and *ālu šá* ^{kur}*gu-ti-i* (l.9').

16.   The reading *ú-lim-ma*, he went away up, is doubtful, but cf. BM. 25124, 21 (Wiseman 1956, 74).

17.   zah or possibly *ha-a-it-'* (*ha'attu*, 'faintness', WO 3 (1964), 48ff.).

Rev.

6.   *Aliksandaris* restored after l. 11; cf. *Iraq* 16 (1954), 203 (BM. 35603, Seleucid King List, 5); Smith 1924, 141 (BM. 34660+36313, r.14 (both '*a-lik-sa-an-dar*).

10.   Possibly uzu.me.zé?

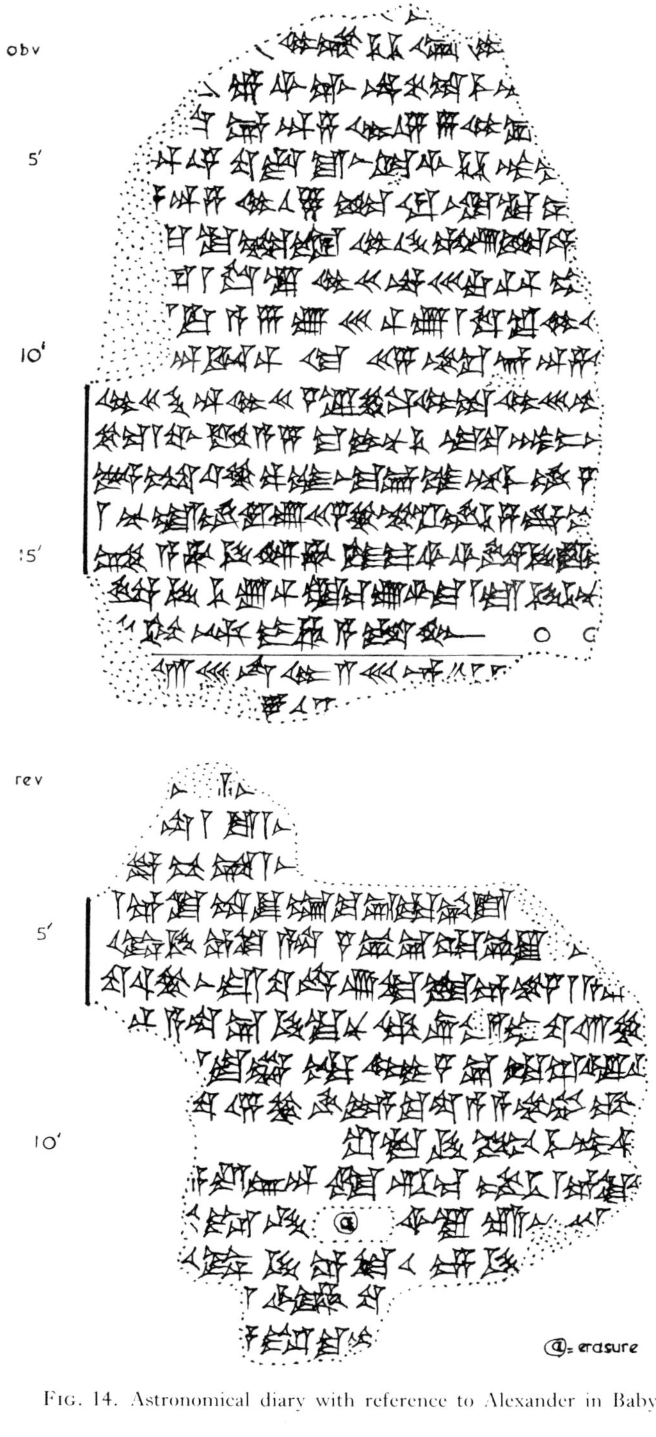

FIG. 14. Astronomical diary with reference to Alexander in Babylon

BIBLIOGRAPHY

AHARONI, Y., 1975. *Investigations at Lachish*.
———— 1981. *Arād Inscriptions*. Jerusalem.
AHMED, S.S., 1968. *Southern Mesopotamia in the time of Ashurbanipal*. Paris.
ALBRIGHT, W.F., 1956. 'The Nebuchadnezzar and Neriglissar Chronicles', in *BASOR* 143, 28–33.
ALI, S.M., 1979. 'The Southern Palace', in *Sumer* 35, 92–3.
AL-KASSAR, A., 1981. 'The Procession Street', in *Sumer* (forthcoming: Papers read at the Babylon Symposium, Baghdad, 1981).
AVIGAD, N., 1979. 'Jerahmeel and Baruch', in *BA* 42, 114–17.
BARNETT, R.D., 1958. 'Early Shipping in the Near East', in *Antiquity* 32, 220–30.
———— 1963. 'Xenophon and the Wall of Media', in *JHS* 83, 1–26.
———— 1976. *Sculptures from the North Palace of Ashurbanipal at Nineveh*. London.
———— 1982. 'A Note on the Paleo-Hebrew and Neo-Hebrew Scripts', in *Eretz Israel* 16, 1–6.
BARTLETT, J.R., 1982. 'Edom and the Fall of Jerusalem, 587 B.C.' in *PEQ* 114, 13–24.
BELJAWSKI, V.A., 1971. 'Der politische Kampf in Babylon in den Jahren 562–556 v. Chr.', in M. Lurker (ed.), *Beiträge zu Geschichte, Kultur und Religion des alten Orients* (in memoriam E. Unger), 197–215.
BEN-BARAK, Z., 1980. 'The Coronation Ceremonies of Joash and Nabopolasar in Comparison', in B. Oded (ed.), *Studies in the History of the Jewish People and the Lands of Israel*, 5, 43–56.
———— 1980A. 'The Coronation Ceremony in Ancient Mesopotamia', in *Orientalia Lovaniensia Periodica* 11, 55–67.
BERGAMINI, G., 1977. 'Levels of Babylon Reconsidered', in *Mesopotamia* 12, 111–52.
BERGER, P–R., 1973. *Die neubabylonischen Königsinschriften: Königsinschriften des ausgehenden babylonischen Reiches (626–539 a. Chr.)*. (*AOAT* 4/1) Kevelaer.
———— 1975. 'Der Kyros-Zylinder mit den Zusatzfragment BIN II Nr. 32 und die akkadischen Personennamen im Danielbuch', in *ZA* 64, 192–234.
BIGGS, R.D., 1967. 'More Babylonian "Prophecies"', in *Iraq* 29, 117–32.

———— 1969. 'Medicine in Ancient Mesopotamia', in *History of Science* 8, 44–105.

BORGER, R., 1956. *Die Inschriften Asarhaddons Königs von Assyrien*. Graz.

BRAUN, T.F.B.G., 1982. 'The Neo-Babylonian Empire and the Greeks', in J. Boardman and N.G.L. Hammond (ed.), *Cambridge Ancient History* III, Pt. 3, 21–4.

BRIGHT, J., 1965. *Jeremiah* (Anchor Bible, 21).

BRINKMAN, J.A., 1964. 'Merodach-baladan II' in R.M. Adams (et al. ed.) *Studies Presented to A. Leo Oppenheim June 7, 1964*, 16–53.

———— 1966. 'Neo-Babylonian Texts in the Archaeological Museum at Florence', in *JNES* 25, 202–9.

———— 1968. *A Political History of Post-Kassite Babylonia 1158–722 B.C. (An.Or. 43)*.

———— 1973. 'Sennacherib's Babylonian Problem: An Interpretation', in *JCS* 25, 89–95.

———— 1977. 'Notes on the Arameans and Chaldeans in Southern Babylonia in the Early Seventh Century B.C.', in *Or* 46, 304–25.

———— 1979. 'Babylonia under the Assyrian Empire, 745–627 B.C.', in M.T. Larsen (ed.) *Power and Propaganda. A Symposium on Ancient Empires*, 223–50.

BURSTEIN, S.M., 1978. *The babyloniaca of Berossus*. (SANE I/5 Malibu).

CAVIGNEAUX, A. 1981. 'Le Temple de Nabû ša harê: Rapport préliminaire sur les textes cunéiformes', in *Sumer* 37 (1981), 118–26.

———— 1981A. 'Les textes cunéiformes sur Babylone', in *Histoire et Archéologie* 51 (March 1981), 35–7.

CLINES, D.J.A., 1972. 'Regnal Year Reckoning in the last Years of the Kingdom of Judah', in *Australian Journal of Biblical Archaeology*, 2, 9–34.

COXON, P.W., 1976. 'Greek Loan Words and alleged Greek Loan Traditions in the Book of Daniel', in *Transactions of the Glasgow University Oriental Society* 25 (1973/4, published 1976), 24–40.

CROWN, A.D., 1974. 'Tidings and Instructions: How News Travelled in the Ancient Near East', in *JESHO* 17, 244–71.

DAMERJI, M.S., 1981. 'Babylone; les familles nouvelles et les travaux de restauration' in *Histoire et Archéologie* 51 (1981), 26–34.

———— 1981A. 'Where are the Hanging Gardens of Babylon?', *Sumer* 37 (1981) 56–61 (Arabic).

DANDAMAYEV, M.A., 1980. 'About Life Expectancy in Babylonia in the first millennium B.C.' in B. Alster (ed.), *Death in Mesopotamia* (Copenhagen), 183–6.

———— 1982. 'The Neo-Babylonian Elders', in *Societies and Lan-*

guages of the Ancient Near East; Studies in Honour of I.M. Diakonoff (Warminster, 1982), 38–41.

———— 1982A. 'The Social Position of Neo-Babylonian Scribes', in Schriften zur Geschichte und Kultur des alten Orient 15 (1982), 35–9.

———— 1983. 'Nādin, a Scribe of the Eanna Temple', AfO Beih. 19 (1983), 400–2.

DEGEN, R., 1972. Neue Ephemeris für Semitische Epigraphik I,

DIETRICH, M., 1970. Die Aramäer Südbabyloniens in der Sargonidenzeit (700–648).

DOSSIN, G., 1981. 'Marduk, Dieu Poliade de Babylone', Akkadica 22 (1981), 1–2.

DOUGHERTY, R.P., 1923. Archives from Erech, Time of Nebuchadnezzar and Nabonidus (Goucher College Cuneiform Inscriptions I).

———— 1929. Nabonidus and Belshazzar (YOSR XV).

———— 1933. Archives from Erech, Neo-Babylonian and Persian Periods (Goncher College Cuneiform Inscriptions II).

DRIOTON, E. & VANDIER, J., 1952. L'Egypte.

DRIVER, G.R., 1955. 'Neo-Babylonian Laws' in The Babylonian Laws II, 324–47.

———— 1976. Semitic Writing from Pictograph to Alphabet.

DUMBRELL, W.J., 1972. 'Jeremiah 49:28–33; An Oracle against a proud desert Power', in Australian Journal of Biblical Archaeology 2, 99–109.

EDZARD, D.O. & FARBER, G., 1974. Répertoire Géographique des Textes Cunéiformes, Band 2.

EISSFELDT, O., 1933. 'Das Datum der Belagerung von Tyrus durch Nebukadnezzar', in Forschungen und Fortschritte (= Kleine Schrift II, 1–3). 9, 421–2.

ELAT, M., 1982. 'Mesopotamische Königsrituale', in Bi.Or. 39, 6–26.

ELLIS, R.S., 1968. Foundation Deposits in Ancient Mesopotamia (YNER 2).

EPH'AL, I., 1979. 'Israel: Fall and Exile' in WHJP I, 276–89.

———— 1982. The Ancient Arabs (Nomads on the Borders of the Fertile Crescent: 9th–5th Centuries B.C.).

FENSHAM, F.C., 1982. 'Nebukadrezzar in the Book of Jeremiah', in JNWSL 10, 53–65.

FERRARA, A.J., 1975. 'An Inscribed Stone Slab of Nebuchadnezzar' in JCS 27, 231–2.

FREEDY, K.S. & REDFORD, D.B., 1970. 'The Dates in Ezekiel in Relation to Biblical, Babylonian and Egyptian Sources', in JAOS 90, 426–85.

FUNCK, B., 1982. 'Studien zur sozialökonomischen Situation Babyloniens im 7. und 6. Jahrhundert v.u.Z.', in Schriften zur

Geschichte und Kultur der alten Orient 15 (1982), 45–67.

GADD, C.J., 1948. *Ideas of Divine Rule in the Ancient East.*

————— 1958. 'The Harran Inscriptions of Nabonidus', in *An.St.* 8, 35–92.

————— 1967. 'Omens expressed in numbers', in *JCS* 21, 52–63.

GARELLI, P., 1981. 'La conception de la royauté en Assyrie', in F.M. Fales (ed.), *Assyrian Royal Inscriptions: New Horizons*, 1–11.

GELB, I.J., 1955. 'The Name of Babylon', in *Journal of the Institute of Asian Studies* I, 1–4.

GEORGE, A.R., 1979. 'The Cuneiform Text tin.tir.ki=*Ba-bi-lu* and the Topography of Babylon', in *Sumer* 35, 226–32.

GEVA, H., 1979. 'The Western Boundary of Jerusalem at the End of the Monarchy', in *IEJ* 29, 84–91.

GIBSON, J.C.L., 1975. *Aramaic Inscriptions (Text-book of Syrian Semitic Inscriptions 2).*

GIBSON, M. & BIGGS, R.D., 1977. *Seals and Sealing in the Ancient Near East* (= SSANE).

GLAESEMAN, R.A., 1978. *The Practise of the King's Meal in Mari: A System of Food Distribution in the 2nd. millennium B.C.* (Ph.D. Dissertation, University of California, Los Angeles).

GOETZE, A., 1946. 'A Cylinder of Nebuchadrezzar from Babylon', in *Crozier Quarterly* 23/1, 65–78.

GRAYSON, A.K. & LAMBERT, W.G., 1964. 'Akkadian Prophecies', in *JCS* 18, 7–30.

GRAYSON, A.K., 1972. *Assyrian Royal Inscriptions, Part I. (From the Beginning to Assur-resha-ishi I)*, 1972.

————— 1975. *Assyrian and Babylonian Chronicles.*

————— 1975A. *Babylonian Historical-Literary Texts.*

————— 1976. *Assyrian Royal Inscriptions, Part 2, (From Tiglath-pileser I to Ashur-nasir-apli II).*

GREENFIELD, J., 1982. 'Babylonian Aramaic Relationship' in H.J. Nissen & J. Renger (ed.), *Mesopotamien und seine Nachbarn* II, 471–82.

GRELOT, P., 1979. 'L'Orchestre de Daniel III 5, 7, 10, 15' in *VT* 29, 23–38.

GURNEY, O.R., 1974. 'The Fifth Tablet of "The Topography of Babylon"', in *Iraq* 36, 39–52.

HALLO, W.W., 1966. 'Akkadian Apocalypses', in *IEJ* 16, 231–42.

————— 1971, (with W.K. Simpson). *The Ancient Near East: A History.*

————— 1982. 'Nebukadnezar Comes to Jerusalem', in J.V. Plant (ed.), *Through The Sound of Many Voices: Writings Contributed on occasion of the 70th. Birthday of W. Gunther Plant*, 40–56.

HARTMAN, L.F., 1962. 'The Great Tree and Nabuchodonosor's Madness' in J.L. McKenzie (ed.), *The Bible in Current Roman*

Catholic Thought, 75–82.

HORN, S.H., 1967. 'The Babylonian Chronicle and the Ancient Calendar of the Kingdom of Judah', in *Andrews University Seminary Studies* 3, 12–27.

———— 1968. 'Where and when was the Aramaic Saqqara Papyrus Written?', in *Andrews University Seminary Studies* 6, 29–45.

HUNGER, H., 1968. *Babylonische und assyrische Kolophone* (= AOAT 2).

———— 1975, (with KAUFMAN, S.A.). 'A New Akkadian Prophecy Text', in *JAOS* 95, 371–5.

———— 1976. *Spätbabylonische Texte aus Uruk I.*

IRA, S., 1972. *Studies in Neo-Babylonian Economic and Legal Texts* (University of Minnesota Ph. D. dissertation).

JOANNÈS, F., 1980. 'Kaššaia, fille de Nabuchodonsor II' in *RA* 74, 183–4.

———— 1982. 'La Location de Ṣurru à l'époque néo-babylonienne', in *Semitica* 32 (1982), 35–42.

JOHNS, C.H.W., 1989. *Assyrian Deeds and Documents* I (1898), II (1901), III (1901), IV (1923).

JONGELING, B., LABUSCHAGNE, C.J., VAN DER WONDE, A.S., 1976. *Aramaic Texts from Qumran I*, 123–31.

KAMEL, A., 1979. 'The Inner Wall of Babylon', *Sumer* 35, 148–9.

KATZENSTEIN, S.J., 1973. *The History of Tyre.*

———— 1983. 'Before Pharaoh conquered Gaza', in *VT* 33, 249–51.

KENYON, K., 1967. *Jerusalem.*

KHALIL, B. & CAVIGNEAUX, A., 1981. 'Les textes cunéiformes sur Babylone', in *Histoire et Archéologie* 51, 35–7.

KIENITZ, F.K., 1967. *Die Säitische Renaissance* in E. Cassin (et. al. ed.) Die Altorientalischen Reiche III (= Fischer Weltgeschichte IV, 256–81 4, 269.

KING, L.W., 1907. *Chronicles Concerning Early Babylonian Kings*

———— 1912. *Babylonian Boundary Stones and Memorial – Tablets in the British Museum.*

KINNIER WILSON, J.V., 1967. 'Mental Diseases of Ancient Mesopotamia' in D. Brothwell and A.T. Sandison (ed.), *Diseases in Antiquity*, 723–33.

———— 1972. *The Nimrud Wine Lists* (Cuneiform Texts from Nimrud II).

KITCHEN, K.A., 1970. 'Ancient Orient, "Deuteronism," and the Old Testament', in J. Barton Payne (ed.), *New Perspectives in the Old Testament*, 1–24.

———— 1973. *The Third Intermediate Period in Egypt.*

KÖCHER, F., 1963. *Die babylonisch-assyrische Medizin in Texten und Untersuchungen* I (1963); V–VI (1980).

KOLDEWEY, R., 1911. *Die Tempel von Babylon und Borsippa.*

———— 1914. *The Excavations at Babylon* (trans. A.S. Johns).

————— 1932. *Die Königsburgen von Babylon*: II Die Hanptburg und der Sommerpalast Nebukadnezars im Hügel Babil (= *WVDOG* 55).

KRISCHEN, F., 1956. *Weltwunder der Baukunst in Babylonien und Jonien*.

LABAT, R., 1935. *Le poème babylonien de la Création*.

————— 1960. 'Ordonnances medicales ou magiques', in *RA* 54, 169–76.

LAMBERT, W.G., 1960. *Babylonian Wisdom Literature*.

————— 1964. 'The Reign of Nebuchadnezzar I: A Turning Point in the History of Ancient Mesopotamian Religion', in W.S. McCullough (ed.), *The Seed of Wisdom: Essays in Honour of T.J. Meek*, 3–13.

————— 1965. 'Nebuchadnezzar King of Justice', in *Iraq* 27, 1–11.

————— 1966. *Enuma eliš, The Babylonian Epic of Creation*.

————— 1974. 'The Seed of Kingship', in P. Garelli (ed.), *Le Palais et la royauté*, 432–4.

————— 1978. *The Background of Jewish Apocalyptic* (Ethel M. Wood Lecture, University of London, 22 February 1977).

————— 1982. 'The Interchange of Ideas between Southern Mesopotamia and Syria-Palestine as seen in Literature', in H-J. Nissen and J. Renger (ed.), *Mesopotamien und seine Nachbarn* I, 311–16.

LANGDON, S.H., 1912. *Die neubabylonischen Königsinschriften* (= VAB IV Leipzig).

LARSEN, M.T., 1979. 'The Tradition of Empire in Mesopotamia', in *Power and Propaganda: A Symposium on Ancient Empires*, 75–103.

LEEMANS, W.F., 1946. 'Kidinnu. Un symbole de droit divin Babylonien' in M. David (et. al. ed.) *Symbolae ad Jus et Historiam Antiquitatis Pertinentes Julio Christiano van Oven Dedicatae*, 36–61 (Leiden).

LEVY, S.J., 1947. 'Two Cylinders of Nebuchadnezzar II in the Iraq Museum', in *Sumer* 3, 4–18.

LIPIŃSKI, E., 1972. 'The Eygpto-Babylonian War of the winter of 601–600 B.C.', in *Annali dell'Istituto Orientale di Napoli* 32, 235–41.

————— 1975. *Studies in Aramaic Inscriptions and Onomastics* (Orientalia Lovanensia Analecta I).

LÖWINGER, S., 1948. 'Nebuchadnezzar's Dream in the Book of Daniel' in *Ignace Goldziher Memorial Volume I* (Budapest–Jerusalem) 336–52.

LUCKENBILL, D.D., 1924. *The Annals of Sennacherib*.

LUTZ, H.F., 1927. *Neobabylonian Administrative Documents from Erech*. (Berkeley).

MALAMAT, A., 1956. 'A New Record of Nebuchadrezzar's

Palestinian Campaigns', in *IEJ* 6, 246–55.

———— 1968. 'The Last Kings of Judah and the Fall of Jerusalem', in *IEJ* 18, 138–56.

———— 1971. 'Exiles in Assyria', in *Encyclopedia Judaica* 6, 1074–6.

———— 1973. 'Josiah's Bid for Armageddon. The Background of the Judean–Egyptian Encounter in 609 B.C.' in *Journal of the Ancient Near Eastern Society of Columbia University* 5, 267–78.

———— 1979. 'The Last Years of the Kingdom of Judah', in *World History of the Jewish People*, 205–21.

MAZAR, A, 1981. 'Khirbet Abu et-Twein and the system of Iron Age Fortresses in Judah' in *Eretz Israel* 15, 229–49.

McEWAN, G.J., 1982. *The Late Babylonian Tablets in the Royal Ontario Museum* (Royal Ontario Museum Cuneiform Texts. Vol. II).

MILIK, J.T., 1967. 'Les papyrus araméens d'Hermopolis et les cultes syro-phéniciens en Égypte' in *Biblica* 48, 546–62.

MILLARD, A.R., 1977. 'Daniel 1–6 and History' in *Evangelical Quarterly* 49 (1977) 71–2.

———— (with A. Abou-Assaf & P. Bordreuil), 1982. *La Statue de Tell Fekherye et son inscription bilingue assyro-araméenne*.

———— 1983. 'Assyrians and Arameans', in *Iraq* 45, 101–8.

MITCHELL, T.C. and JOYCE, R., 1965. 'The Musical Instruments in Nebuchadrezzar's Orchestra' in D.J. Wiseman (ed.), *Notes on Some Problems in the Book of Daniel*, 19–27.

MOORE, E.W., 1935. *Neo-Babylonian Business and Administrative Documents*.

———— 1939. *Neo-Babylonian Documents in the University of Michigan Collection*.

MÜLLER, K.F., 1937. 'Das assyrische Ritual' in *MVAG* 41/3, 4–19.

NASIR, M., 1979. 'The Temple of Ishtar of Agad', in *Sumer* 35, 78–81.

NASSOUHI, E., 1926. 'Deux Vases Royaux Néobabyloniens', in *AfO* 3, 65–6.

NEMET-NEJAT, K., 1982. *Late Babylonian Field Plans in The British Museum* (Studia Pohl: Series Maior 11).

NOTH, M., 1958. 'Die Einnahme von Jerusalem im Jahre 597 v.Chr.' in *ZDPV* 74, 133–57.

NÖTSCHER, R., 1957. '"Neue" babylonische Chroniken und Altes Testament' in *Biblische Zeitschrift* 1, 110–14.

ODED, B., 1977. 'Judah and the Exile', in M. Hayes and J.M. Miller, *Israelite and Judean History*, 435–88.

———— 1979. *Mass Deportations and Deportees in the Neo-Assyrian Empire* (Wiesbaden).

OLMSTEAD, A.T., 1925. 'The Chaldean Dynasty', in *HUCA* 2, 29–55.

OPPENHEIM, A.L., 1955. '"Siege-Documents" from Nippur', in *Iraq* 17, 68–89.

———— 1956. *The Interpretation of Dreams in the Ancient Near East.*

———— 1962. 'Mesopotamian Medicine', in *Bulletin of the History of Medicine* 36/2, 97–108.

———— 1964. *Ancient Mesopotamia.*

———— 1965. 'On Royal Gardens in Mesopotamia', in *JNES* 24, 328–33.

———— 1969. 'Divination and Celestial observation in the last Assyrian Empire', in *Centaurus* 14, 97–135.

PARKER, R.A. and DUBBERSTEIN, W.H., 1956. *Babylonian Chronology 626 B.C.–A.D. 75.*

PARPOLA, S., 1970. *Letters from Assyrian Scholars to the Kings Esarhaddon and Assurbanipal.*

———— 1970A. *Neo-Assyrian Toponyms (AOAT 6).*

PARROT, A., 1949. *Ziggurats et Tour de Babel.*

PAYNE, J.B., 1970, *New Perspectives in the Old Testament* (Texas).

PINCHES, T.G., 1902. *The Old Testament in the Light of the Historical Records of Assyria and Babylonia.*

———— 1982. *Cuneiform Texts from Babylonian Tablets in the British Museum: Neo-Babylonian and Achaemenid Texts. Parts 55–57.*

PORTEN, B., 1980. 'Aramaic Letters: A Study in Papyrological Reconstruction' in *Journal of the American Research Center in Egypt* 17, 39–75.

———— 1981. 'The Identity of King Adon' in *BA* 44, 36–59.

PORTEOUS, N., 1965. *Daniel: A Commentary.* 1965.

POSTGATE, J.N., 1973. *The Governor's Palace Archive* (Cuneiform Texts from Nimrud I).

———— 1974. 'The Royal Exercise of Justice under The Assyrian Empire', in P. Garelli (ed.), *Le palais et la royauté* (Paris), 417–26.

QUINN, J.D., 1961. 'Alcaeus 48 (B16) and the fall of Ascalon (604 B.C.), in *BASOR* 164, 19–20.

RAINEY, A.F., 1975. 'The Fate of Lachish during the Campaigns of Sennacherib and Nebuchadrezzar', in Y. Aharoni (ed.), *Investigations at Lachish*, 47–60.

RAVN, O.E., 1942. *Herodotus' Description of Babylon.*

RENGER, J., 1979. 'The City of Babylon during the Old Babylonian period', in *Sumer* 35, 205–9.

REVIV, H., 1985. 'Kidinnu: Observations on Privileges of Mesopotamian Cities', (forthcoming).

ROBERTS, J.J.M., 1977. 'Nebuchadnezzar's Elamite Crisis in theological Perspective', in M. de J. Ellis (ed.), *Essays on the*

Ancient Near East in memory of J.J. Finkelstein, 183–7.

ROSNER, F., 1978. *Julius Preuss' Biblical and Talmudic Medecine*.

SACHS, A.J., 1948. 'A Classification of the Babylonian Astronomical Tablets of the Seleucid Period,' in *JCS* 2, 271–90.

———— 1952. 'Babylonian Horoscopes', in *JCS* 6, 49–75.

———— 1955. *Late Babylonian Astrological & Related Texts* (copied by T.G. Pinches and J.N. Strassmaier).

———— 1974. 'Babylonian observational astronomy', in F.R. Hodson (ed.), *The Place of Astronomy in the Ancient World*, 43–50.

SACK, R.H., 1972. *Amēl-Marduk 562–560 B.C.* (AOATS 4).

———— 1978. 'Nergal-šarra-uṣur, King of Babylon as seen in the Cuneiform, Greek, Latin and Hebrew sources,' in *ZA* 68, 129–49.

———— 1982. 'Nebuchadnezzar and Nabonidus in Folklore and History', in *Mesopotamia* 17, 67–131.

SAGGS, H.W.F., 1962. *The Greatness that was Babylon*.

SAN NICOLÒ, M., 1941. *Beitrage zur einer Prosopographie neubabylonischer Beamten der Zivil- und Tempelverwaltung*.

SCHMIDT, E.F., 1953. *Persepolis I* (O.I.P. 68).

SCHMIDT, H., 1981. 'Ergebnisse einer Grabung am Kernmassiv der Ziggurat in Babylon' in *Baghdader Mitteilungen* 12, 87–137.

SHERIFFS, D.C.T., 1976. *Empire and the gods: Mesopotamian Treaty Theology and the Sword in the First Millennium B.C.* (D.Lit. Thesis, University of Stellenbosch).

SMITH, S., 1924. *Babylonian Historical Texts*.

SOLLBERGER, E., 1979. 'Babylon's Beginnings' in *IInd International Symposium on Babylon* (unpublished).

SPALINGER, A., 1977. 'Egypt and Babylonia: A Survey (c. 620 B.C.–550 B.C.)', in *Studien zur altägyptischen Kultur*, 221–44.

STAMM, J.J., 1939. *Die akkadische Namengebung* (= MVAeG 44).

STARKY, J., 1960. 'Une tablette araméene de l'an 34 de Nabuchodonosor (AO.21.063)', in *Syria* 37, 99–115.

STRASSMAIER, J.N., 1889. *Inschriften von Nabuchodonosor König von Babylon* (Babylonische Texte, Heft V–VI, Nos. 1–460).

STRECK, M., 1916. *Assurbanipal und die letzten assyrischen Könige bis zum untergange Niniveh's*.

SWAIN, J.W., 1940. 'The Theory of Four Monarchies: Opposition History under the Roman Empire', in *Classical Philology* 35, 1–21.

TADMOR, H., 1956. 'Chronicles of the Last Kings of Judah', in *JNES* 15, 226–30.

———— 1982. 'The Aramaization of Assyria: Aspects of Western Impact', in H.J. Nissen and J. Renger (ed.), *Mesopotamien und seine Nachbarn II*, 449–70.

TALLQVIST, K.L., 1906. *Neubanylonisches Namenbuch* (Acta Societatis Scientiarium Fennicae 42.2: Helsingfors).

THIELE, E.R., 1956. 'New Evidence on the Chronology of the Last Kings of Judah', in *BASOR* 143, 22–37.

THUREAU-DANGIN, F., 1907. *Die sumerischen und akkadischen Königsinschriften* (= VAB I)

————— 1912. *Une relation de la huitième campagne de Sargon.*

————— 1921. *Rituels Accadiens.*

TRENKVALDER, H., 1979. 'Some remarks on the place name Babil', in *Sumer* 35, 237–40.

TSEVAT, M., 1959. 'The Neo-Assyrian and Neo-Babylonian Vassaloaths and the prophet Ezekiel', in *JBL* 78, 199–204.

UNGER, E., 1926. 'Nebukadnezar II und sein *sandabaku* (Oberkommisar) in Tyrus', in *ZATW* 3, 314–17.

————— 1928. 'Babylon', in *RlA* I, 330–69.

————— 1931. *Babylon, die heilige Stadt nach der Beschreibung der Babylonier.*

UNGNAD, A., 1937. in M. San Nicolò & A. Ungnad, *Neubabylonische Rechts- und Verwaltungsurkunden I.* Glossar.

VAN SELMS, A., 1974. 'The Name Nebuchadnezzar' in M.S.H.G. Heerma van Voss (et.al.ed.), *Travels in the World of the Old Testament* (Studies Presented to Professor M.A. Beek on the occasion of his 65th Birthday).

VATTIONI, F., 1970. 'Epigrafia Aramaica', in *Augustiniarum* 10, 493–532.

VOGT, E., 1957. 'Die neubabylonische Chronik über die schlacht bei Karkemisch und die Einnahme von Jerusalem' in *Supp. V.T.* 4, 67–96.

————— 1958. 'Der Nehar Kebar: Ez. 1' in *Biblica* 39, 211–16.

VON SODEN, W., 1971. 'Etemenanki von Asarhaddon nach der Erzahlung vom Turmbau zu «Babel und dem Erra-Mythos"', in *UF* 3, 253–63.

VON VOIGTLANDER, E.N., 1964. *A Survey of Neo-Babylonian History* (Ph.D. dissertation, University of Michigan 1963).

————— 1978. *The Bisitun Inscription of Darius the Great: Babylonian Version* (Corpus Inscriptionum Iranicarum I.II.1).

WALKER, C.B.F., 1981. *Cuneiform Brick Inscriptions in The British Museum; The Ashmolean Museum, Oxford; The City of Birmingham Museums and Art Gallery; The City of Bristol Museum and Art Gallery.*

WEIDNER, E.F., 1939. 'Jojachin, König von Juda, in babylonischen Keilschrifttexten' in *Mélanges Syriens offerts à Monsieur René Dussaud II*, 923–35.

————— 1953. note in *AfO* 16, Tf. XVII (after p. 424).

————— 1954. 'Hochverrat gegen Nebukadnezar II', in *AfO* 17 (1954/5), 1–5.

WEINFELD, M., 1976. 'The Loyalty-oath in the Ancient Near East' in *UF* 8, 379–414.

WEISBERG, D.B., 1974. 'Royal Women of the Neo-Babylonian period', in P. Garelli (ed.), *Le palais et la royauté* (Compte rendu de la XIXe RAI, Paris 1974), 447–54.

———— 1980 *Texts from the Time of Nebuchadnezzar* (YOS XVIII).

———— 1982. 'Wool and Linen Material in Texts from the Time of Nebuchadnezzar', in *Eretz Israel* 16, 218–26.

WEISSBACH, F.H., 1906. *Die Inschriften Nebukadnezars II im Wadi Brissa und am Nahr el-kelb* (WVDOG V).

WETZEL, F., 1930. *Die Stadtmauern von Babylon* (WVDOG 48).

————, and WEISSBACH, F.H., 1938. *Das Hauptheiligtum des Marduk in Babylon, Esagila und Etemenanki* (WVDOG 59).

WISEMAN, D.J., 1952. 'A New Stela of Aššur-naṣir-pal II', in *Iraq* 14, 24–44.

———— 1956. *Chronicles of Chaldaean Kings (626–556 B.C.) in The British Museum*.

———— 1958. *The Vassal-Treaties of Esarhaddon* (= *Iraq* 20, 1–99; pls. 1–53).

———— 1962. 'The Laws of Hammurabi Again', in *JSS* 7, 161–72.

———— 1965. *Notes on Some Problems in the Book of Daniel* (Tyndale Press, London).

———— 1966. 'Some Egyptians in Babylonia', in *Iraq* 28, 154–58.

———— 1967. 'A Late Babylonian tribute list?', in *Bulletin of the School of Oriental & African Studies* 30 pt. 3, 495–504.

———— 1972. 'A Babylonian Architect?', in *An.St.* 22, 141–7.

———— 1973. 'Law and Order in Old Testament Times', in *Vox Evangelica* 8, 5–21.

———— 1975. 'Assyria and Babylonia *c.* 1200–1000 B.C.' in *Cambridge Ancient History* II.2, 443–81.

———— 1977. Review of Grayson 1975 in *Bi.Or.* 34, 335–6.

———— 1979. 'Jonah's Nineveh', in *Tyndale Bulletin* (Cambridge) 30, 29–51.

———— 1979A. 'Babylon and Ashur: Centres of Ancient Learning', in Paper read at the Second Symposium on Babylon, Ashur and Hamrin, Baghdad, Sept. 26–Oct. 7, 1979 (to be published).

———— 1980. 'Abraham Reassessed', in A.R. Millard and D.J. Wiseman (ed.), *Essays on the Patriarchal Narratives*, 139–56.

———— 1981. Review of Weisberg 1980, in *Bulletin of the School of Oriental & African Studies* 44.3, 567.

———— 1982. '"Is it Peace?" – Covenant and Diplomacy', in *VT* 32, 311–26.

———— 1983. 'Mesopotamian Gardens', in *An. St.* 33 (1983) 137–44.

WOOLLEY, C.L., 1921. *Carchemish II: The Town Defences*.

ZADOK, R., 1977. *On West Semites in Babylonia during the Chaldean and Achaemenian Periods.*

————— 1978. 'Phoenicians, Philistines and Moabites in Mesopotamia', in *BASOR* 230, 57–65.

————— 1978A. 'The Nippur Region during the late Assyrian, Chaldean and Achaemenid Periods Chiefly from Written Sources', in *Israel Oriental Studies* 8, 266–332.

————— 1979. *The Jews in Babylonia during the Chaldaean and Achaemenian Periods.*

————— 1981. 'Babylonian Notes: 1. The Neo/Late Babylonian Pronunciation of the Divine Names', in *Bi.Or.* 38, 547–9.

—————, 1981A. 'Toponomy of the Nippur Region during the First Millennium B.C. within the general framework of Mesopotamian Topography', in *WO* 12 (1981) 39–69.

————— 1982. 'Notes on the Early History of the Israelites and Judeans in Mesopotamia', in *Or* 51, 391–3.

ZAWADSKI, S.T., 1979. 'The Economic crisis in Uruk during the Last Years of Assyrian rule in the light of the Nabu-ušallim Archives', in *Folia Orientalia* 20, 175–84.

INDEX

I. GENERAL

II. AKKADIAN WORDS & SUMEROGRAMS

III. ARAMAIC, HEBREW, GREEK etc

IV. BIBLICAL REFERENCES